W9-BZV-443

all recipes™ tried & true

quick & easy

top 200 recipes

all recipes™ tried & true

quick & easy

top 200 recipes

all recipes™

Published by Allrecipes.com, Inc.
524 Dexter Ave. N., Seattle, WA 98109
(206) 292-3990

Copyright © 2002 by Allrecipes. All rights reserved.
No part of this book may be reproduced or utilized in any form or by any means, electronic or mechanical, or by any information storage or retrieval system, without written permission from the publisher.

Allrecipes, Allrecipes.com, and Cookierecipe.com are trademarks or registered trademarks of Allrecipes.com, Inc.

For distribution information, contact Allrecipes.

Printed in the U.S.A.
First Edition June 2002

Library of Congress Cataloging-in-Publication data is on file with the publisher.

10 9 8 7 6 5 4 3 2 1

ISBN 0-9711-7232-3

EDITOR: Tim Hunt
SENIOR RECIPE EDITOR: Syd Carter
SENIOR FOOD EDITOR: Jennifer Anderson
PRODUCTION MANAGER: Jill Charing
RECIPE EDITORS: Emily Brune, Richard Kozel, Britt Swearingen
CREATIVE DIRECTION: Yann Oehl
DESIGN: Jeff Cummings
ILLUSTRATION: Richard Ruiz

Cover photograph copyright 2002, The Reuben Group

Recipe shown on cover: *Suki's Spinach and Feta Pasta* (113)

dedication

· ·

This book is dedicated to working
parents who heroically bring home the
bacon, then manage to find the time to
fry it up in a pan....

acknowledgments

The book you are holding is a community cookbook: the recipes within come from the community of cooks who gather online at Allrecipes.com. It is the members of this community, first and foremost, who we would like to thank - anyone that has shared, reviewed, requested, or tried an Allrecipes recipe. The success of the Allrecipes community resides in your experience, enthusiasm, and generosity.

In addition, a huge debt of thanks is owed to the staff of Allrecipes - the people who have dedicated themselves to building a helpful, supportive environment for our community.

table of contents

introduction

what's for dinner?

Do these three little words cause a pang of fear to run through you? Are you too often tempted to order pizza rather than face the steaming stovetop after a long, hard day? Let's face it: The universal need for quick and easy recipes long ago became the rule, not the exception. After all, love is not measured by hours spent in the kitchen so much as by the moments enjoyed while settled at the dinner table. Relying on speedy, simple recipes isn't "cheating," it's your best bet for really having it all — the satisfaction of serving a wholesome and tasty home-cooked meal without dread, plus more time left to do things that really matter to you. That's why we've put together an entire book of our very best quick and easy meals for you.

what is "quick and easy," anyway?

All of the recipes in this book can be prepared from start to finish in an hour or less, from the moment you flip to the recipe you want, to the moment you're dishing it onto outstretched plates. No overnight marinating or long hours waiting for things to simmer slowly. In the back of the book on page 272, you'll find an index of all the recipes sorted by total preparation time. On those nights when time is at a premium, it will help you find something that can be on the table in 15 minutes; when you have a little more time to breathe, you can choose from the dishes at the other end of the timetable. Some of the recipes with longer prep times do have more chopping and mixing involved, while others are just as straightforward as the quickies but simply take a little longer to cook.

stay flexible

One of the cardinal rules of kitchen survival is to stay flexible in your cooking. If you find yourself lacking (or disliking) ingredients in a recipe — substitute! Use another shape of pasta, an alternate vegetable, a different stock or broth, or some other variety of cheese. When you don't have or don't care for the specific kind of meat or seafood called for in a recipe, you'll find it usually works just as well with a replacement, or in many cases, with tofu or beans too. Be ready to improvise, and always taste as you cook. Too bland? Add some salt and pepper. Need a little kick? Add vinegar or lemon juice or hot sauce. Need more texture? Top with toasted bread crumbs or chopped nuts. You can make nearly every recipe meet your needs.

keeping things "quick" and "easy"

Speedy and simple cooking is a state of mind. A few moments spent organizing will save lots of time and effort. Double up on your tasks: Your stove has at least two burners and one oven, so use them! Boil the pasta while you're making the sauce, steam the rice while you're stirring the stir-fry, and bake the potatoes while you're searing the steak. Long-term planning can save even more time. Since it's just as easy to roast two chickens (or hams, or pot roasts...) as it is to roast *one*, get in the habit of cooking "planned leftovers." Chop up and freeze in meal-size portions anything you're not going to eat in the next few days. The makings of your next pasta dish, casserole, soup or sandwich will be waiting for you.

thawing meat

In the refrigerator: Plan ahead, as this is the slowest thawing technique. Small frozen items may thaw overnight in the refrigerator, while larger items will take significantly longer.

In cold, running water: Place the frozen food in a leak-proof bag and place it under cold running water.

In a microwave on the defrost setting: Plan to cook the food immediately after it has thawed in a microwave, because some areas of the food may have begun cooking during the defrost cycle.

the well-stocked pantry

There are times when a trip to the grocery store may as well be an expedition to a distant planet — you're too tired, too hungry, or too crunched for time. This is when your well-stocked pantry saves the day. A pantry is not so much a specific place in the kitchen as it is a mind-set. Even if you don't have a spacious, shelf-lined closet in the kitchen, see to it that you always have a selection of canned and packaged ingredients, as well as spices, seasonings and accompaniments. Always think of your pantry as a work in progress: Add a few items each shopping trip and restock items as you run low. Many items have long shelf lives, so they'll be ready when you need them. Buy meat in bulk and freeze in meal-size portions. Buy your dry goods in bulk and repackage in airtight containers. Knowing you've got the makings for a million-and-one quick dinners at home will help you resist the temptation of the fast food drive-through window forever more.

recipe tips

variations on a theme

You may wonder why we have more than one recipe for some items, such as potato soup or chicken salad or stuffed peppers. Don't worry — these are far from being duplicates. Some dishes are so popular that our community members share multiple variations of them. As we post new versions of a recipe, we may add a Roman numeral to the title to distinguish it from another (for example, the "Broccoli Cheese Soup III" recipe which appears in this book). There are lots of different ways to approach even the old standards, and in this book you can enjoy your next meal of stuffed peppers with a down-home filling of ground beef, mushrooms and gravy, or with a light and tangy interior of Arborio rice, feta cheese and fresh tomatoes. Come see us at Allrecipes.com to explore new renditions of *all* your old favorites.

about the recipes

Half the fun of an Allrecipes recipe is the story behind it — each of our recipes has comments submitted by the contributor to help explain how the recipe came about, what it's like, or how they use it. As the editors of the Allrecipes cookbooks, both online and in print, the staff works hard to preserve the character of the contributed recipe, but also strives to ensure consistency, accuracy, and completeness in the published version and throughout the collection.

all in the timing

At the top right corner of every recipe in the book, you'll find "Preparation," "Cooking," and "Ready In" times. These numbers are approximate! Depending on how fast you chop vegetables, how quick you are with a can opener, and whether or not you take advantage of convenience products like pre-shredded cheese, bagged salad greens and pre-cooked chicken, you may find that it takes less or more time than we've estimated. The "Ready In" times will tell you, on average, how much time the recipe takes from start to finish. With a few recipes, this will be slightly longer than the "Preparation" time plus the "Cooking" time. These are recipes that contain intermediate steps that aren't prepping or cooking, such as waiting for the meat to marinate for a few minutes. Refer to the "Ready In" time to know roughly how long you need between opening the book and serving the finished dish.

need help? we're here for you!

Need more information about an unfamiliar ingredient or cooking term, general cooking information, or difficult techniques? We've got a whole section of Allrecipes.com dedicated to giving you all the help you need. In our "Cooking Basics" section, you can search for thousands of kitchen terms, follow photo-filled step-by-step tutorials to learn important cooking skills, and browse or search hundreds of articles that will help you decide what to make and teach you how to make it. You can access the "Cooking Basics" section at Allrecipes: **http://allrecipes.com/cb/**

beyond the book

Each of the recipes in this book can be accessed online at Allrecipes.com. The online versions have some handy, whiz-bang features we didn't manage to squeeze into this book. If you'd like to adjust the number of servings for a recipe, view detailed nutritional information, convert the measurements to metric, or email a copy to a friend, it's all just a click away! The online version also includes user reviews that often come with variations and handy tips. We've created a special place on Allrecipes.com where you can find any recipe in this book simply by entering its page number. Check it out! **http://allrecipes.com/tnt/qandez/page.asp**

your two cents

Once you try a recipe in this book, you can tell the rest of the world all about it! First, locate the recipe on Allrecipes.com (see above). Next, click on the link that says "Add to Recipe Box" (below the recipe's description). Then, follow the instructions to set up a FREE recipe box of your own. Once you've added the recipe to your box, you can rate it on a scale of 1 to 5 stars and share your comments with the millions of other people who use the site. Come tell us what you think!

tried & true

If you'd like to find out more about this book, the recipes, and other Allrecipes "tried & true" cookbooks - join us online at **http://allrecipes.com/tnt/** or send us an email at **tnt@allrecipes.com**

salads

Speed up your salads by using those handy bags of pre-washed, pre-trimmed greens. They cost a little more, but the time you save may be worth the money. When you prepare salad dressing, fix a big batch — most varieties of dressing will keep for several weeks in the refrigerator. Think it takes too long to cut up all those vegetables? Try having your kitchen knives sharpened; you'll be amazed at how much quicker — and more fun — it is to use a functioning blade.

Caesar Salad Supreme

Submitted by: **Karen Weir**

Makes: 6 servings

Preparation: 20 minutes

Cooking: 15 minutes

Ready In: 35 minutes

"A wonderful, rich, anchovy dressing makes this salad a meal. Serve with crusty Italian Bread."

INGREDIENTS

6 cloves garlic, peeled

¾ cup mayonnaise

5 anchovy fillets, minced

6 tablespoons grated Parmesan cheese, divided

1 teaspoon Worcestershire sauce

1 teaspoon Dijon mustard

1 tablespoon lemon juice

salt to taste

ground black pepper to taste

¼ cup olive oil

4 cups day-old bread, cubed

1 head romaine lettuce, torn into bite-size pieces

DIRECTIONS

1. Mince 3 cloves of garlic, and combine in a small bowl with mayonnaise, anchovies, 2 tablespoons of the Parmesan cheese, Worcestershire sauce, mustard, and lemon juice. Season to taste with salt and black pepper. Refrigerate until ready to use.

2. Heat oil in a large skillet over medium heat. Cut the remaining 3 cloves of garlic into quarters, and add to hot oil. Cook and stir until brown, and then remove garlic from pan. Add bread cubes to the hot oil. Cook, turning frequently, until lightly browned. Remove bread cubes from oil, and season with salt and pepper.

3. Place lettuce in a large bowl. Toss with dressing, remaining Parmesan cheese, and bread cubes.

Classic Tossed Salad

Submitted by: **Toni Bankson**

Makes: 12 servings

Preparation: 20 minutes

Cooking: 10 minutes

Ready In: 30 minutes

"This is a delicious salad that goes great with any meal, especially Italian!"

INGREDIENTS

1 cup blanched slivered almonds

2 tablespoons sesame seeds

1 head romaine lettuce, torn into bite-size pieces

1 head red leaf lettuce, torn into bite-size pieces

1 (8 ounce) package crumbled feta cheese

1 (4 ounce) can sliced black olives

1 cup cherry tomatoes, halved

1 red onion, halved and thinly sliced

6 fresh mushrooms, sliced

¼ cup grated Romano cheese

1 (8 ounce) bottle Italian salad dressing

DIRECTIONS

1. Heat a large skillet over medium-high heat. Place the almonds in the skillet, and cook, stirring frequently until lightly browned. When the almonds are beginning to turn, add sesame seeds, and cook 1 more minute, or until seeds are toasted.

2. In a large salad bowl, combine lettuce with feta cheese, olives, almonds, sesame seeds, tomatoes, onion, mushrooms, and Romano cheese. When ready to serve, toss with Italian dressing.

Green Salad with Cranberry Vinaigrette

Submitted by: **Nancy**

Makes: 8 servings

Preparation: 15 minutes

Cooking: 5 minutes

Ready In: 20 minutes

"Green salad that is especially pretty to serve during the Christmas holidays."

INGREDIENTS

1 cup sliced almonds

3 tablespoons red wine vinegar

1/3 cup olive oil

1/4 cup fresh cranberries

1 tablespoon Dijon mustard

1/2 teaspoon minced garlic

1/2 teaspoon salt

1/2 teaspoon ground black pepper

2 tablespoons water

1/2 red onion, thinly sliced

4 ounces crumbled blue cheese

1 pound mixed salad greens

DIRECTIONS

1. Preheat oven to 375°F (190°C). Arrange almonds in a single layer on a baking sheet. Toast in oven for 5 minutes, or until nuts begin to brown.

2. In a blender or food processor, combine the vinegar, oil, cranberries, mustard, garlic, salt, pepper, and water. Process until smooth.

3. In a large bowl, toss the almonds, onion, blue cheese, and greens with the vinegar mixture until evenly coated.

Mandarin Orange, Gorgonzola and Almond Delight

Makes: 6 servings

Preparation: 15 minutes

Cooking: 5 minutes

Ready In: 20 minutes

Submitted by: **Paula Wilson**

"This is an easy and flavorful citrus salad. The cheese makes it great, so use as much as you wish."

INGREDIENTS

½ cup blanched slivered almonds

1 (11 ounce) can mandarin oranges, juice reserved

2 tablespoons vegetable oil

2 tablespoons red wine vinegar

12 ounces mixed salad greens

1 cup Gorgonzola cheese

DIRECTIONS

1. Heat a skillet over medium-high heat. Add almonds, and cook, stirring frequently, until lightly toasted. Remove from heat, and set aside.

2. In a small bowl, whisk together 2 tablespoons reserved mandarin orange juice, oil, and vinegar.

3. In a large salad bowl, toss together the toasted almonds, mandarin oranges, mixed salad greens, and Gorgonzola cheese. Just before serving, pour dressing on salad, and toss to coat.

Field Salad

Submitted by: **Candice Brosnan**

Makes: 4 servings

Preparation: 10 minutes

Ready In: 10 minutes

"This easy salad recipe will thrill all of your guests! Field greens are not just for the home gardener anymore. Commercial mesclun, a mixture of young, crisp, greens, is becoming a year-round staple. Adorn this nice salad with fresh herbs and edible flowers for an extra special treat."

INGREDIENTS

8 ounces mixed salad greens

3/4 cup chopped walnuts

8 ounces Gorgonzola cheese, crumbled

2 tart green apples, cored and diced

1/2 (8 ounce) bottle raspberry vinaigrette salad dressing

DIRECTIONS

1. In a large bowl, combine salad greens, walnuts, cheese, and apples. Toss with raspberry vinaigrette, and serve.

Strawberry Romaine Salad II

Submitted by: **Dort**

Makes: 6 servings

Preparation: 15 minutes

Ready In: 15 minutes

"This is a great summer salad that utilizes fresh romaine, onions, strawberries, and a sweet poppy seed dressing."

INGREDIENTS

1 head romaine lettuce, torn into bite-size pieces

1 red onion, sliced

1 pint fresh strawberries, sliced

1 (11 ounce) can mandarin oranges

1 cup mayonnaise

2 tablespoons maraschino cherry juice

2 tablespoons honey

1 tablespoon poppy seeds

⅛ teaspoon lemon juice

DIRECTIONS

1. In a large bowl, mix the romaine lettuce, red onion, strawberries, and mandarin oranges.

2. In a medium bowl, whisk together the mayonnaise, cherry juice, honey, poppy seeds, and lemon juice. Pour over the lettuce mixture, and toss to coat.

Spinach and Strawberry Salad

Submitted by: **Jerry Lynne**

Makes: 8 servings

Preparation: 10 minutes

Ready In: 10 minutes

"My family loves this all year round if we can find strawberries. Even the grandchildren love this salad. Quick and easy."

INGREDIENTS

2 bunches spinach, rinsed and torn into bite-size pieces

4 cups sliced strawberries

1/2 cup vegetable oil

1/4 cup white wine vinegar

1/2 cup white sugar

1/4 teaspoon paprika

2 tablespoons sesame seeds

1 tablespoon poppy seeds

DIRECTIONS

1. In a large bowl, toss together the spinach and strawberries.

2. In a medium bowl, whisk together the oil, vinegar, sugar, paprika, sesame seeds, and poppy seeds. Pour over the spinach and strawberries, and toss to coat.

Jamie's Cranberry Spinach Salad

Submitted by: **Jamie Hensley**

Makes: 8 servings

Preparation: 10 minutes

Cooking: 10 minutes

Ready In: 20 minutes

"Everyone I have made this for RAVES about it! It's different and so easy to make!"

INGREDIENTS

1 tablespoon butter

3/4 cup blanched and slivered almonds

1 pound spinach, rinsed and torn into bite-size pieces

1 cup dried cranberries

2 tablespoons toasted sesame seeds

1 tablespoon poppy seeds

1/2 cup white sugar

2 teaspoons minced onion

1/4 teaspoon paprika

1/4 cup white wine vinegar

1/4 cup cider vinegar

1/2 cup vegetable oil

DIRECTIONS

1. In a medium saucepan, melt butter over medium heat. Cook and stir almonds in butter until lightly toasted. Remove from heat, and let cool.

2. In a large bowl, combine the spinach with the toasted almonds and cranberries.

3. In a medium bowl, whisk together the sesame seeds, poppy seeds, sugar, onion, paprika, white wine vinegar, cider vinegar, and vegetable oil. Toss with spinach just before serving.

Harvest Salad

Submitted by: **Tiffany**

Makes: 6 servings

Preparation: 15 minutes

Ready In: 15 minutes

"Spinach salad with blue cheese, walnuts, and dried cranberries. If you can't find walnut oil, olive oil may be substituted."

INGREDIENTS

1/2 cup chopped walnuts

1 bunch spinach, rinsed and torn into bite-size pieces

1/2 cup dried cranberries

1/2 cup crumbled blue cheese

2 tomatoes, chopped

1 avocado - peeled, pitted and diced

1/2 red onion, thinly sliced

2 tablespoons red raspberry jam (with seeds)

2 tablespoons red wine vinegar

1/3 cup walnut oil

freshly ground black pepper to taste

salt to taste

DIRECTIONS

1. Preheat oven to 375°F (190°C). Arrange walnuts in a single layer on a baking sheet. Toast in oven for 5 minutes, or until nuts begin to brown.

2. In a large bowl, toss together the spinach, walnuts, cranberries, blue cheese, tomatoes, avocado, and red onion.

3. In a small bowl, whisk together jam, vinegar, walnut oil, pepper, and salt. Pour over the salad just before serving, and toss to coat.

Wilted Spinach Salad

Submitted by: **Chip**

Makes: 12 servings

Preparation: 30 minutes

Cooking: 15 minutes

Ready In: 45 minutes

"An interesting salad that is definitely not low cal! Very popular as a side dish or a meal with my family and friends."

INGREDIENTS

6 eggs

1 pound bacon

2 bunches fresh spinach, rinsed and dried

4 green onions, thinly sliced

2 eggs

¼ cup white sugar

¼ cup white vinegar

¼ cup red wine vinegar

DIRECTIONS

1. Place 6 eggs in a medium saucepan with enough cold water to cover. Bring water to a boil, and immediately remove from heat. Cover, and let eggs stand in hot water for 10 to 12 minutes. Remove from hot water, cool, peel, and chop.

2. Place bacon in a large, deep skillet. Cook over medium high heat until evenly brown. Drain, crumble, and set aside, reserving approximately ½ cup of drippings in the skillet.

3. In a large bowl, toss together the spinach and green onions.

4. Heat the reserved drippings over low heat. In a small bowl, whisk together the 2 remaining eggs, sugar, white vinegar, and red wine vinegar. Add to warm grease, and whisk for about a minute, until thickened. Pour at once over spinach, add crumbled bacon, and toss to coat. Garnish with chopped egg.

Amby Rae's Cucumber Salad

Submitted by: Amber Smith

Makes: 6 servings

Preparation: 15 minutes

Ready In: 15 minutes

"This is my simplest and easiest recipe yet for cucumber salad, my specialty! If you're not a sour cream fan, substituting plain yogurt works great."

INGREDIENTS

2 large cucumbers, peeled and cubed

2 cups sour cream

4 sprigs fresh mint, chopped

3 cloves garlic, peeled and minced

¼ cup lemon juice

¼ cup olive oil

¼ teaspoon salt

⅛ teaspoon ground black pepper

DIRECTIONS

1. Place cucumbers in a large salad bowl, and set aside.

2. In a small bowl, whisk together the sour cream, mint, garlic, lemon juice, olive oil, salt, and pepper until well blended. Pour over the cucumbers, and mix until well coated.

Cucumber and Tomato Salad

Submitted by: **Tigrgrrl**

Makes: 4 servings

Preparation: 15 minutes

Ready In: 15 minutes

"A refreshing, light salad for any hot, humid summer day! The kidney beans and tofu make it a great main dish for vegetarians, as well. The basil may be substituted with fresh parsley or mint. Be sure to make this salad just before serving."

INGREDIENTS

1 tomato, chopped

1 cucumber, seeded and chopped

1/4 cup thinly sliced red onion

1/4 cup canned kidney beans, drained

1/4 cup diced firm tofu

2 tablespoons chopped fresh basil

1/4 cup balsamic vinaigrette salad dressing

salt and pepper to taste

DIRECTIONS

1. In a large bowl, combine the tomato, cucumber, red onion, kidney beans, tofu, and basil. Just before serving, toss with balsamic vinaigrette salad dressing, and season with salt and pepper.

Crispy Cucumbers and Tomatoes in Dill Dressing

Submitted by: **Michele O'Sullivan**

Makes: 6 servings

Preparation: 15 minutes

Ready In: 30 minutes

"Crispy cucumbers, fresh tomatoes, and onion add spark to this simple summer salad."

INGREDIENTS

¼ cup cider vinegar

1 teaspoon white sugar

½ teaspoon salt

½ teaspoon chopped fresh dill weed

¼ teaspoon ground black pepper

2 tablespoons vegetable oil

2 cucumbers, sliced

1 cup sliced red onion

2 ripe tomatoes, cut into wedges

DIRECTIONS

1. In a large bowl, mix the vinegar, sugar, salt, dill, pepper, and oil. Add cucumbers, onion, and tomatoes. Toss, and let stand at least 15 minutes before serving.

Mediterranean Greek Salad

Submitted by: **Heather Shevlin**

Makes: 8 servings

Preparation: 10 minutes

Ready In: 10 minutes

"This is a great salad to take to a barbeque. All ingredients are approximate, so add more or less of any ingredient depending on your own taste."

INGREDIENTS

3 cucumbers, seeded and sliced

1½ cups crumbled feta cheese

1 cup black olives, pitted and sliced

3 cups diced roma tomatoes

⅓ cup diced oil packed sun-dried tomatoes, drained, oil reserved

½ red onion, sliced

DIRECTIONS

1. In a large salad bowl, toss together the cucumbers, feta cheese, olives, roma tomatoes, sun-dried tomatoes, 2 tablespoons reserved sun-dried tomato oil, and red onion. Chill until serving.

Broccoli Salad

Submitted by: **Jennifer Stephens**

Makes: 8 servings

Preparation: 15 minutes

Cooking: 15 minutes

Ready In: 30 minutes

"This nutty and fruity broccoli salad is a big hit at potlucks! The recipe was given to me by my Aunt Rossanne. She is the best cook ever! To bulk up the salad, you can add an extra cup of broccoli."

INGREDIENTS

1 pound bacon

4 cups broccoli florets

5 green onions, chopped

¼ cup sunflower seeds

¼ cup golden raisins

1 cup mayonnaise

½ cup white sugar

6 tablespoons red wine vinegar

DIRECTIONS

1. Place bacon in a large skillet. Cook over medium-high heat until evenly browned. Cool, crumble, and set aside.

2. In a large bowl, toss together broccoli, green onions, sunflower seeds, raisins, and bacon.

3. In a small bowl, mix together mayonnaise, sugar, and red wine vinegar. Toss with vegetables to coat. Cover, and chill until serving.

Sesame Broccoli Salad

Submitted by: **Sara**

Makes: 8 servings

Preparation: 15 minutes

Cooking: 10 minutes

Ready In: 25 minutes

"This bright green salad features blanched broccoli tossed in a light sesame dressing with toasted sesame seeds. Quick and delicious!"

INGREDIENTS

2 tablespoons sesame seeds

1½ pounds fresh broccoli, cut into bite size pieces

2 tablespoons rice vinegar

2 tablespoons soy sauce

2 tablespoons sesame oil

2 teaspoons white sugar

DIRECTIONS

1. Preheat oven to 375°F (190°C). Toast sesame seeds for 3 to 5 minutes, or until the seeds begin to turn golden brown. Set aside.

2. Bring a large pot of water to a boil. Cook broccoli in boiling water for 3 to 5 minutes, or until desired tenderness. Drain, and transfer to a large bowl.

3. In a small bowl, whisk together the vinegar, soy sauce, sesame oil, sugar, and sesame seeds. Pour over broccoli, and toss to coat.

Asian Coleslaw

Submitted by: **Bobbi Ritcheske**

Makes: 10 servings

Preparation: 30 minutes

Ready In: 30 minutes

"A great twist on cabbage salad. The peanut butter in the dressing is the secret."

INGREDIENTS

6 tablespoons rice wine vinegar

6 tablespoons vegetable oil

5 tablespoons creamy peanut butter

3 tablespoons soy sauce

3 tablespoons brown sugar

2 tablespoons minced fresh ginger root

1½ tablespoons minced garlic

5 cups thinly sliced green cabbage

2 cups thinly sliced red cabbage

2 cups shredded napa cabbage

2 red bell peppers, thinly sliced

2 carrots, julienned

6 green onions, chopped

½ cup chopped fresh cilantro

DIRECTIONS

1. In a medium bowl, whisk together the rice vinegar, oil, peanut butter, soy sauce, brown sugar, ginger, and garlic.

2. In a large bowl, mix the green cabbage, red cabbage, napa cabbage, red bell peppers, carrots, green onions, and cilantro. Toss with the peanut butter mixture just before serving.

Egg Salad III

Submitted by: **Stacey**

Makes: 2 cups

Preparation: 15 minutes

Cooking: 10 minutes

Ready In: 25 minutes

"This is a great egg salad recipe that a woman I babysat for made! The key ingredient is the chopped pimento stuffed olives. Serve on toasted bread with lettuce and a bit of chopped celery."

INGREDIENTS

8 eggs

½ cup mayonnaise

1 teaspoon ground black pepper

¼ teaspoon paprika

2 tablespoons pimento-stuffed green olives, chopped

DIRECTIONS

1. Place eggs in a medium saucepan with enough cold water to cover, and bring to a boil. Cover saucepan, remove from heat, and let eggs stand in hot water for 10 to 12 minutes. Remove from hot water, cool, peel, and chop.

2. In a large bowl, mix eggs, mayonnaise, pepper, and paprika. Mash with a potato masher or fork until smooth. Gently stir in the olives. Refrigerate until serving.

Carol's Chicken Salad

Submitted by: **Sharon Sisson**

Makes: 8 servings

Preparation: 20 minutes

Ready In: 20 minutes

"My friend Carol is a wonderful cook, and this recipe is a '10.' By far the best chicken salad I have tasted."

INGREDIENTS

1/2 cup mayonnaise

1/2 teaspoon salt

3/4 teaspoon poultry seasoning

1/4 teaspoon onion powder

1/4 teaspoon garlic powder

1/4 teaspoon ground black pepper

1 tablespoon lemon juice

3 cups diced, cooked chicken breast meat

1/2 cup finely chopped celery

1/2 cup chopped green onions

1 (8 ounce) can water chestnuts, drained and chopped

1 1/2 cups diced Swiss cheese

1 1/2 cups halved green grapes

DIRECTIONS

1. In a medium bowl, whisk together the mayonnaise, salt, poultry seasoning, onion powder, garlic powder, pepper, and lemon juice.

2. In a large bowl, toss together the chicken, celery, green onions, water chestnuts, Swiss cheese, and grapes. Add the mayonnaise mixture, and stir to coat. Chill until serving.

Best Chicken Salad Ever

Submitted by: **Samantha**

Makes: 6 servings

Preparation: 10 minutes

Ready In: 10 minutes

"This is the result of a day at home with my brother and nothing to do. We decided to create a new lunch. Serve on rolls or sandwich bread; this is especially nice if you toast the bread, or use a flavorful whole-grain bread. The chicken can be substituted with turkey, and the ingredients can be rearranged to suit differing tastes. Enjoy!"

INGREDIENTS

1 (5 ounce) can chunk chicken, drained and flaked

2 tablespoons creamy salad dressing

1 teaspoon sweet pickle relish

1 large apple, cored and diced

1 cup chopped pecans

1/2 stalk celery, chopped (optional)

2/3 cup raisins

salt and pepper to taste

DIRECTIONS

1. In a large bowl, mix the chicken, creamy salad dressing, pickle relish, apple, pecans, celery, and raisins. Season with salt and pepper. Chill until serving.

Curry Chicken Salad

Submitted by: **Samantha**

Makes: 6 servings

Preparation: 10 minutes

Ready In: 10 minutes

"A cold chicken salad spread ideal for a sandwich. Serve on bread with lettuce, and enjoy!"

INGREDIENTS

3 cooked skinless, boneless chicken breast halves, chopped

3 stalks celery, chopped

1/2 cup low-fat mayonnaise

2 teaspoons curry powder

DIRECTIONS

1. In a medium bowl, stir together the chicken, celery, mayonnaise, and curry powder.

Hawaiian Chicken Salad

Submitted by: **Shirlie Burns**

Makes: 6 servings

Preparation: 10 minutes

Ready In: 10 minutes

"This delicious, fruity chicken salad is a change from the standard. It's easy to double the recipe for a larger group."

INGREDIENTS

2 (3 ounce) packages cream cheese, softened

1/3 cup creamy salad dressing, e.g. Miracle Whip ™

1 (8 ounce) can pineapple tidbits, juice reserved

3 (5 ounce) cans chunk chicken, drained

1 cup blanched slivered almonds

1 1/2 cups seedless grapes, halved

DIRECTIONS

1. In a medium bowl, beat cream cheese until fluffy. Mix in salad dressing and 2 tablespoons reserved pineapple juice. Stir in the pineapple tidbits, chicken, almonds, and grapes until evenly coated. Chill until serving.

Sesame Pasta Chicken Salad

Submitted by: Olivia Hines

Makes: 10 servings

Preparation: 20 minutes

Cooking: 10 minutes

Ready In: 30 minutes

"A refreshing light pasta salad with a delicious Asian flair. Great for a summer cookout or picnic. Tastes great right away, and even better if you can allow it to marinate for a while."

INGREDIENTS

1/4 cup sesame seeds

1 (16 ounce) package bow tie pasta

1/2 cup vegetable oil

1/3 cup light soy sauce

1/3 cup rice vinegar

1 teaspoon sesame oil

3 tablespoons white sugar

1/2 teaspoon ground ginger

1/4 teaspoon ground black pepper

3 cups shredded, cooked chicken breast meat

1/3 cup chopped fresh cilantro

1/3 cup chopped green onion

DIRECTIONS

1. Heat a skillet over medium-high heat. Add sesame seeds, and cook stirring frequently until lightly toasted. Remove from heat, and set aside.

2. Bring a large pot of lightly salted water to a boil. Add pasta, and cook for 8 to 10 minutes, or until al dente. Drain pasta, and rinse under cold water until cool. Transfer to a large bowl.

3. In a jar with a tight-fitting lid, combine vegetable oil, soy sauce, vinegar, sesame oil, sugar, sesame seeds, ginger, and pepper. Shake well.

4. Pour sesame dressing over pasta, and toss to coat evenly. Gently mix in chicken, cilantro, and green onions.

Bob's Thai Beef Salad

Submitted by: **John Dimmick**

Makes: 4 servings

Preparation: 20 minutes

Cooking: 10 minutes

Ready In: 30 minutes

"Unique taste of Thai. Blend of flavors is truly unbelievable. You must try for yourself. WOW! We suggest serving over white rice. Any other way would not be Bob's way."

INGREDIENTS

1 pound beef rib eye steak

2 large cucumbers - peeled, halved lengthwise and sliced

2 red onions, halved and thinly sliced

15 Thai chiles, sliced into thin rings

3 limes, juiced

1 pinch white sugar

1 cup fish sauce

DIRECTIONS

1. Preheat oven to broiler setting. Broil rib eye to desired doneness. When cool enough to handle, slice into ¼ inch by 1 inch strips.

2. In a large bowl, combine the steak, cucumbers, onions, chiles, lime juice, sugar, and fish sauce. Stir gently for 5 minutes, or until flavors are well blended.

Italian Taco Salad

Submitted by: **Blayne**

Makes: 6 servings

Preparation: 15 minutes

Cooking: 10 minutes

Ready In: 25 minutes

"This is a quick and easy salad with lots of taste. Great for a chip dip also."

INGREDIENTS

1 pound ground beef

3 cups crushed tortilla chips

2 cups shredded mozzarella cheese

2 cups shredded Cheddar cheese

1 (10 ounce) package mixed salad greens

1 (8 ounce) bottle zesty Italian dressing

DIRECTIONS

1. In a medium skillet over medium heat, cook the ground beef until evenly browned. Remove from heat, and drain.

2. In a large bowl, combine the ground beef, tortilla chips, mozzarella cheese, Cheddar cheese, and salad greens. Toss with Italian dressing until evenly coated, and serve.

Fatoosh

Submitted by: **Winna**

Makes: 6 servings

Preparation: 20 minutes

Cooking: 10 minutes

Ready In: 30 minutes

"Sumac is available at Middle Eastern food stores. It may be left out of this salad, but the flavor to me is important to the overall taste."

INGREDIENTS

2 pita breads

8 leaves romaine lettuce, torn into bite-size pieces

2 green onions, chopped

1 cucumber, chopped

3 tomatoes, cut into wedges

1/4 cup chopped fresh parsley

1 clove garlic, peeled and chopped

2 tablespoons sumac powder

1/4 cup lemon juice

1/4 cup olive oil

1 teaspoon salt

1/4 teaspoon ground black pepper

1/4 cup chopped fresh mint leaves

DIRECTIONS

1. Preheat oven to 350°F (175°C).

2. Toast pitas 5 to 10 minutes in the preheated oven, until crisp. Remove from heat, and break into bite size pieces.

3. In a large bowl, toss together toasted pita pieces, romaine lettuce, green onions, cucumber, and tomatoes.

4. In a small bowl, mix the parsley, garlic, sumac powder, lemon juice, olive oil, salt, pepper, and mint. Pour over the pita mixture, and toss just before serving.

Orzo and Tomato Salad with Feta Cheese

Submitted by: **Sabrina Harris**

Makes: 6 servings

Preparation: 15 minutes

Cooking: 10 minutes

Ready In: 25 minutes

"A cold pasta salad with orzo, green olives, feta cheese, parsley, dill, tomato, olive oil, and lemon juice. If you don't have fresh herbs, use dried, but be sure to use more to make up the difference in flavor. As a personal chef, I can let you know that my clients love this dish."

INGREDIENTS

1 cup uncooked orzo pasta

¼ cup pitted green olives

1 cup diced feta cheese

3 tablespoons chopped fresh parsley

3 tablespoons chopped fresh dill

1 ripe tomato, chopped

¼ cup virgin olive oil

⅛ cup lemon juice

salt and pepper to taste

DIRECTIONS

1. Bring a large pot of lightly salted water to a boil. Cook orzo for 8 to 10 minutes, or until al dente; drain, and rinse with cold water.

2. When orzo is cool, transfer to a medium bowl and mix in olives, feta cheese, parsley, dill, and tomato. In a small bowl, whisk together oil and lemon juice. Pour over pasta, and mix well. Season with salt and pepper to taste. Chill before serving.

Chickpea Macaroni Salad

Submitted by: **Christine**

Makes: 6 servings
Preparation: 10 minutes
Cooking: 10 minutes
Ready In: 50 minutes

"This Greek-style pasta salad would also be good tossed with fresh avocado and mint."

INGREDIENTS

1 cup macaroni

1 (19 ounce) can chickpeas (garbanzo beans), drained

4 tomatoes, chopped

1 onion, chopped

1 clove garlic, minced

6 ounces feta cheese, crumbled

1 cup pitted black olives

1 teaspoon salt

1/2 teaspoon ground black pepper

1/2 cup olive oil

1/4 cup fresh lemon juice

DIRECTIONS

1. Bring a medium saucepan of lightly salted water to a boil. Add macaroni, and cook 8 to 10 minutes, or until al dente. Rinse under cold water to chill, and drain.

2. Meanwhile, combine the chickpeas, tomatoes, onion, garlic, feta cheese, olives, salt, pepper, olive oil, and lemon juice in a large bowl. Set aside to marinate while the pasta is cooking.

3. Mix macaroni with chickpea mixture. Cover, and refrigerate for at least 30 minutes to blend flavors.

Easy Bean Salad

Submitted by: **Kathi S.**

Makes: 12 servings

Preparation: 10 minutes

Ready In: 10 minutes

"An easy, delicious, cold bean salad. A big hit at barbeques and football parties! Use any 3-bean combination. Red beans are also really nice in this salad!"

INGREDIENTS

1 (15 ounce) can black beans, drained and rinsed

1 (15 ounce) can garbanzo beans, drained and rinsed

1 (15 ounce) can cannellini beans, drained and rinsed

1 (8 ounce) can water chestnuts, drained and chopped

3/4 cup salsa

1/4 cup fat free French dressing

1/2 teaspoon garlic powder

salt and pepper to taste

DIRECTIONS

1. In a large bowl, toss together the black beans, garbanzo beans, cannellini beans, water chestnuts, salsa, and dressing. Season with garlic powder, and salt and pepper. Cover, and chill until serving.

Baja Bean Salad

Submitted by: **Christine Johnson**

Makes: 8 servings

Preparation: 20 minutes

Ready In: 20 minutes

"A simple and tasty south of the border bean salad!"

INGREDIENTS

1 (15 ounce) can kidney beans, drained

1 (15 ounce) can garbanzo beans, drained

1 cup chopped tomatoes

¾ cup cucumber - peeled, seeded, and chopped

2 tablespoons diced onion

1 (6 ounce) container guacamole

½ cup plain yogurt

¼ teaspoon salt

¼ cup milk

shredded lettuce

corn tortilla chips

DIRECTIONS

1. In a large bowl, toss together the kidney beans, garbanzo beans, tomatoes, cucumber, and onion.

2. In a small bowl, mix the guacamole, yogurt, and salt. If dressing seems thick, stir in a little milk. Stir into the bean mixture, and chill. Serve topped with the shredded lettuce and corn chips.

Black Bean Salad

Submitted by: **Merle Shinpoch**

Makes: 12 servings

Preparation: 20 minutes

Ready In: 20 minutes

"This salad is a kaleidoscope of color and taste - black beans, yellow corn, green peppers, and red, red tomatoes. Lime juice, garlic and jalapeno give it some punch. It can also be used as a dip with tortilla chips."

INGREDIENTS

1 (15 ounce) can black beans, rinsed and drained

2 (15 ounce) cans whole kernel corn, drained

8 green onions, chopped

2 jalapeno peppers, seeded and minced

1 green bell pepper, chopped

1 avocado - peeled, pitted, and diced

1 (4 ounce) jar pimentos

3 tomatoes, seeded and chopped

1 cup chopped fresh cilantro

1 lime, juiced

1/2 cup Italian salad dressing

1/2 teaspoon garlic salt

DIRECTIONS

1. In a large bowl, combine the black beans, corn, green onions, jalapeno peppers, bell pepper, avocado, pimentos, tomatoes, cilantro, lime juice, and Italian dressing. Season with garlic salt. Toss, and chill until serving.

Waldorf Salad II

Submitted by: **Penny**

Makes: 4 servings

Preparation: 20 minutes

Ready In: 20 minutes

"This traditional salad is delicious, and you can vary the ingredients to your preference. Try adding diced, roasted chicken to make this salad a meal!"

INGREDIENTS

1/2 cup mayonnaise

1 tablespoon white sugar

1 teaspoon lemon juice

1/8 teaspoon salt

3 apples — peeled, cored, and chopped

1 cup thinly sliced celery

1/2 cup chopped walnuts

1/2 cup raisins (optional)

DIRECTIONS

1. In a medium bowl, whisk together the mayonnaise, sugar, lemon juice, and salt.

2. Stir in the apples, celery, walnuts, and raisins. Chill until ready to serve.

Fabulous Fruit Salad

Submitted by: **Tracy Fall**

Makes: 4 servings

Preparation: 20 minutes

Ready In: 20 minutes

"An easy, quick, and holiday-worthy fruit salad that is easily doubled."

INGREDIENTS

1 red apple, cored and chopped

1 Granny Smith apple, cored and chopped

1 nectarine, pitted and sliced

2 stalks celery, chopped

½ cup dried cranberries

½ cup chopped walnuts

1 (8 ounce) container nonfat lemon yogurt

DIRECTIONS

1. In a large bowl, combine red apple, Granny Smith apple, nectarine, celery, dried cranberries, and walnuts. Mix in yogurt. Chill until ready to serve.

Fruit Salad in Seconds

Submitted by: **Cathy Byron**

Makes: 12 servings

Preparation: 10 minutes

Ready In: 10 minutes

"Caught in a pinch for a salad when unexpected company showed up at mealtime, I improvised with this combination. Instantly it became one of my family's favorites. Best of all, it is quick and easy. You can use lemon yogurt instead of strawberry, if you wish."

INGREDIENTS

1 pint fresh strawberries, sliced

1 pound seedless green grapes, halved

3 bananas, peeled and sliced

1 (8 ounce) container strawberry yogurt

DIRECTIONS

1. In a large bowl, toss together strawberries, grapes, bananas, and strawberry yogurt. Serve immediately.

Vinaigrette

Submitted by: **Karen Castle**

Makes: 1 cup

Preparation: 5 minutes

Ready In: 5 minutes

"This is simple to make and delicious, especially if you like garlic."

INGREDIENTS

½ cup red wine vinegar

½ cup vegetable oil

1 clove crushed garlic

2 teaspoons white sugar

2 teaspoons salt

DIRECTIONS

1. In a jar with a tight fitting lid, combine vinegar, oil, garlic, sugar, and salt. Shake well.

Raspberry Vinaigrette Dressing

Submitted by: **Jan**

Makes: 1½ cups

Preparation: 5 minutes

Ready In: 5 minutes

"This dressing has a mild raspberry flavor. I usually prepare it with canola oil."

INGREDIENTS

½ cup vegetable oil

½ cup raspberry wine vinegar

½ cup white sugar

2 teaspoons Dijon mustard

¼ teaspoon dried oregano

¼ teaspoon ground black pepper

DIRECTIONS

1. In a jar with a tight fitting lid, combine the oil, vinegar, sugar, mustard, oregano, and pepper. Shake well.

Honey Mustard Dressing II

Submitted by: **Mary Ann Benzon**

Makes: 6 tablespoons

Preparation: 5 minutes

Ready In: 5 minutes

"A very old but good recipe. Use as a dip or salad dressing. If you like, you can use lime juice instead of lemon juice."

INGREDIENTS

¼ cup mayonnaise

1 tablespoon prepared mustard

1 tablespoon honey

½ tablespoon lemon juice

DIRECTIONS

1. In a small bowl, whisk together the mayonnaise, mustard, honey, and lemon juice. Store covered in the refrigerator.

Casa Dressing

Submitted by: **Denyse**

Makes: 1 cup

Preparation: 5 minutes.

Ready In: 5 minutes

"Creamy dressing that you sometimes see as the house dressing at Mexican restaurants!"

INGREDIENTS

2/3 cup mayonnaise

1/3 cup milk

1 tablespoon lime juice

1 tablespoon ground cumin

1 teaspoon salt

1 teaspoon ground black pepper

1 tablespoon chopped fresh cilantro

DIRECTIONS

1. In a small bowl, whisk together the mayonnaise, milk, and lime juice. Season with cumin, salt, and pepper. Stir in cilantro just before serving.

Creamy Italian Dressing

Submitted by: **Cathy**

Makes: 1 1/2 cups

Preparation: 10 minutes

Ready In: 10 minutes

"A wonderful, thick dressing - my favorite."

INGREDIENTS

1 cup mayonnaise

1/2 small onion

2 tablespoons red wine vinegar

1 tablespoon white sugar

3/4 teaspoon Italian seasoning

1/4 teaspoon garlic powder

1/4 teaspoon salt

1/8 teaspoon ground black pepper

DIRECTIONS

1. In a blender or food processor, combine mayonnaise, onion, vinegar, and sugar. Season with Italian seasoning, garlic powder, salt, and pepper. Blend until smooth.

Bob's Blue Cheese Dressing

Submitted by: **Bobby Harrison**

Makes: 3 cups

Preparation: 20 minutes

Ready In: 20 minutes

"Prepare a flavorful summer salad by serving this dressing over mixed mesclun greens, hearts of romaine, sliced cucumber, tomato, and red onion."

INGREDIENTS

1 cup crumbled blue cheese

1 cup mayonnaise

1 cup sour cream

2 teaspoons lemon juice

1 teaspoon hot pepper sauce

2 teaspoons Worcestershire sauce

2 tablespoons chopped fresh parsley

1 tablespoon honey

1 teaspoon ground black pepper

1 teaspoon sea salt

DIRECTIONS

1. In a large bowl, whisk together the blue cheese, mayonnaise, sour cream, lemon juice, hot pepper sauce, Worcestershire sauce, parsley, honey, pepper, and salt. Chill until serving.

soups

Soup has a reputation for needing long hours to simmer, but the truth is, you can throw together a marvelous soup in minutes. Warm up some canned broth in a big pot, add frozen vegetables, leftover meat, and maybe some canned tomatoes or beans, seasonings, and you've got dinner! Soup tastes even better the second day, and most soups freeze beautifully, so when you find a recipe you like, make lots!

Rich and Creamy Tomato Basil Soup

Submitted by: **Holly**

Makes: 4 servings

Preparation: 10 minutes

Cooking: 35 minutes

Ready In: 45 minutes

"The secret to the richness of this soup is to use real butter, fresh basil leaves, and heavy cream. Please do not substitute, or you will not have the same high quality end result."

INGREDIENTS

4 tomatoes - peeled, seeded, and diced

4 cups tomato juice

14 leaves fresh basil

1 cup heavy whipping cream

½ cup butter

salt and pepper to taste

DIRECTIONS

1. Place tomatoes and juice in a stock pot over medium heat. Simmer for 30 minutes. Purée the tomato mixture along with the basil leaves, and return the purée to the stock pot.

2. Place the pot over medium heat, and stir in the heavy cream and butter. Season with salt and pepper. Heat, stirring until the butter is melted. Do not boil.

Cream of Fresh Asparagus Soup II

Submitted by: **Holly**

Makes: 4 servings

Preparation: 15 minutes

Cooking: 25 minutes

Ready In: 40 minutes

"There's nothing like fresh asparagus when it's in season - take advantage!"

INGREDIENTS

1 pound fresh asparagus, trimmed and cut into 1 inch pieces

1/2 cup chopped onion

1 (14.5 ounce) can chicken broth

2 tablespoons butter

2 tablespoons all-purpose flour

1 teaspoon salt

1 pinch ground black pepper

1 cup milk

1/2 cup sour cream

1 teaspoon fresh lemon juice

DIRECTIONS

1. In a large saucepan, combine asparagus, chopped onion, and 1/2 cup chicken broth. Cover, and bring to a boil over high heat. Reduce heat, and simmer uncovered until asparagus is tender, about 12 minutes. Process the mixture in a blender to purée the vegetables. Set aside.

2. In the same saucepan, melt the butter over medium-low heat. Stir in the flour, salt, and pepper. Cook, stirring constantly for 2 minutes. Whisk in the remaining chicken broth, and increase the heat to medium. Cook, stirring constantly until the mixture boils. Stir in the asparagus purée and the milk.

3. Put the sour cream in a small bowl, and stir in a ladleful of the hot soup. Add the sour cream mixture and the lemon juice to the soup. Stir while heating the soup to serving temperature, but don't allow it to boil. Serve immediately.

Cauliflower-Cheese Soup

Submitted by: **Jane Snider**

Makes: 4 servings

Preparation: 20 minutes

Cooking: 25 minutes

Ready In: 45 minutes

"A soothing cheesy soup. Serve with a roll and a salad."

INGREDIENTS

3/4 cup water

1 cup cauliflower, chopped

1 cup cubed potatoes

1/2 cup finely chopped celery

1/2 cup diced carrots

1/4 cup chopped onion

1/4 cup butter

1/4 cup all-purpose flour

3 cups milk

salt and pepper to taste

4 ounces shredded Cheddar cheese

DIRECTIONS

1. In a large saucepan, combine water, cauliflower, potatoes, celery, carrots, and onion. Boil for 5 to 10 minutes, or until tender. Set aside.

2. Melt butter in separate saucepan over medium heat. Stir in flour, and cook for 2 minutes. Remove from heat, and gradually stir in milk. Return to heat, and cook until thickened. Stir in vegetables with cooking liquid, and season with salt and pepper. Stir in cheese until melted, and remove from heat.

Broccoli Cheese Soup

Submitted by: **Karin Christian**

Makes: 12 servings

Preparation: 10 minutes

Cooking: 30 minutes

Ready In: 40 minutes

"This is a great, very flavorful soup. Good for serving at luncheons or special gatherings with a quiche. To make this soup a little fancier, add 1 cup sliced mushrooms and 1 cup white wine with the onions."

INGREDIENTS

½ cup butter

1 onion, chopped

1 (16 ounce) package frozen chopped broccoli

4 (14.5 ounce) cans chicken broth

1 (1 pound) loaf processed cheese food, cubed

2 cups milk

1 tablespoon garlic powder

⅔ cup cornstarch

1 cup water

DIRECTIONS

1. In a stockpot, melt butter over medium heat. Cook onion in butter until softened. Stir in broccoli, and cover with chicken broth. Simmer until broccoli is tender, 10 to 15 minutes.

2. Reduce heat, and stir in cheese cubes until melted. Mix in milk and garlic powder.

3. In a small bowl, stir cornstarch into water until dissolved. Stir into soup; cook, stirring frequently, until thick.

Broccoli Cheese Soup III

Submitted by: **Pam Zielinski**

Makes: 12 servings

Preparation: 10 minutes

Cooking: 30 minutes

Ready In: 40 minutes

"A creamy broccoli soup that will please the most fussy eater, even children love it. Complement with crusty Italian bread for a quick, easy meal. For variety, try substituting cauliflower, shredded carrots, or any combination of the three vegetables, keeping the total amount to 4 cups vegetables."

INGREDIENTS

4 cups fresh broccoli, cut into bite size pieces

1½ quarts chicken broth

2 cups milk

2 (10.75 ounce) cans condensed cream of celery soup

4 tablespoons cornstarch

½ cup cold water

2 cups shredded Cheddar cheese

DIRECTIONS

1. In a large soup pot, cook broccoli in broth until tender, about 10 minutes.

2. In a medium bowl, mix together milk and condensed celery soup. Blend cornstarch with cold water, then stir into soup mixture. Pour into the pot with the broccoli. Cook over medium heat, stirring steadily until thick and bubbly. Stir in cheese, and simmer, stirring until hot. Do not boil.

Baked Potato Soup

Submitted by: **Sherry Haupt**

Makes: 6 servings

Preparation: 15 minutes

Cooking: 25 minutes

Ready In: 40 minutes

"Thick and creamy. Uses leftover baked potatoes."

INGREDIENTS

12 slices bacon

2/3 cup margarine

2/3 cup all-purpose flour

7 cups milk

4 large baked potatoes, peeled and cubed

4 green onions, chopped

1 1/4 cups shredded Cheddar cheese

1 cup sour cream

1 teaspoon salt

1 teaspoon ground black pepper

DIRECTIONS

1. Place bacon in a large, deep skillet. Cook over medium heat until browned. Drain, crumble, and set aside.

2. In a stock pot or Dutch oven, melt the margarine over medium heat. Whisk in flour until smooth. Gradually stir in milk, whisking constantly until thickened. Stir in potatoes and onions. Bring to a boil, stirring frequently.

3. Reduce heat, and simmer 10 minutes. Mix in bacon, cheese, sour cream, salt, and pepper. Continue cooking, stirring frequently, until cheese is melted.

Loaded Potato Soup

Submitted by: **Claire**

Makes: 12 servings

Preparation: 15 minutes

Cooking: 15 minutes

Ready In: 30 minutes

"Thick, creamy, potato-y soup! Top with bacon bits and additional grated Cheddar cheese for a flavor explosion!"

INGREDIENTS

8 potatoes, peeled and cubed

½ cup butter

½ cup all-purpose flour

8 cups milk

¼ cup chopped onion

1 (8 ounce) container sour cream

½ cup shredded Cheddar cheese

salt and pepper to taste

DIRECTIONS

1. Place cubed potatoes into a glass dish, and cook in the microwave oven for 7 to 10 minutes, or until soft.

2. While the potatoes are cooking, melt the butter in a large pot over medium-high heat. Whisk in flour until smooth, then gradually stir in the milk. Bring to a boil, then reduce heat to medium, and simmer for 5 to 10 minutes, or until slightly thickened.

3. Stir in the potatoes and onion, and cook for 5 more minutes. Stir in the sour cream and Cheddar cheese until melted and well blended. Season with salt and pepper.

Potato Soup IX

Submitted by: **Carol Hoadley**

Makes: 6 servings

Preparation: 15 minutes

Cooking: 30 minutes

Ready In: 45 minutes

"A delicious soup that makes a meal with some nice fresh bread! Homey and comforting! Try adding shredded Cheddar cheese just before serving."

INGREDIENTS

2 tablespoons butter

1 onion, chopped

2 cloves garlic, minced

5 potatoes, peeled and cubed

2 cups chicken stock

1/4 teaspoon dried thyme

1/2 teaspoon ground black pepper

2 cups milk

salt and pepper to taste

2 tablespoons chopped fresh parsley

DIRECTIONS

1. Melt the butter in a large saucepan over medium heat. Sauté onion and garlic until tender. Add the potatoes, chicken stock, thyme, and pepper. Bring to a boil, then reduce heat to low. Cover, and simmer for 20 minutes, or until potatoes are tender.

2. Transfer about half of the soup to a food processor or blender. Process until smooth, then return to the pot. Stir in milk, and continue cooking until heated through. Season with salt and pepper. Ladle into bowls, and garnish with chopped fresh parsley.

Cream of Spinach Soup

Submitted by: **Joyce Marciszewski**

Makes: 4 servings

Preparation: 5 minutes

Cooking: 20 minutes

Ready In: 25 minutes

"This is a fast, easy way to make creamed soups. You can also use most any frozen vegetable. Cream of broccoli is also delicious."

INGREDIENTS

1½ cups water

3 cubes chicken bouillon

1 (10 ounce) package frozen chopped spinach

3 tablespoons butter

¼ cup all-purpose flour

3 cups milk

1 tablespoon dried minced onion

salt and pepper to taste

DIRECTIONS

1. In a medium saucepan, combine water, bouillon, and spinach. Bring to a boil, and cook until spinach is tender.

2. Melt butter in a large saucepan over medium heat. Stir in flour, and cook for 2 minutes. Gradually whisk in milk. Season with minced onion, salt, and pepper. Cook, stirring constantly, until thickened. Stir in spinach mixture.

Spinach Tortellini Soup

Submitted by: **Nicole**

Makes: 4 servings

Preparation: 5 minutes

Cooking: 15 minutes

Ready In: 20 minutes

"This is a recipe I got from a friend who's in culinary school. It's real simple and tastes even better the next day."

INGREDIENTS

1 (10 ounce) package frozen chopped spinach

2 (14.5 ounce) cans chicken broth

1 (9 ounce) package cheese tortellini

¼ tablespoon dried basil

¼ tablespoon garlic powder

salt and pepper to taste

DIRECTIONS

1. In a large pot over high heat, combine the spinach and chicken broth. Heat to boiling, then reduce heat to low. Stir in tortellini, and simmer for 10 to 15 minutes, or until the tortellini is cooked to desired tenderness. Season with basil, garlic powder, salt, and pepper.

Creamy Mushroom Soup

Submitted by: **Lori**

Makes: 4 servings

Preparation: 10 minutes

Cooking: 15 minutes

Ready In: 25 minutes

"This fresh and creamy soup is easy to make, and filled with hearty chopped mushrooms."

INGREDIENTS

¼ cup butter

1 cup chopped shiitake mushrooms

1 cup chopped portobello mushrooms

2 shallots, chopped

2 tablespoons all-purpose flour

1 (14.5 ounce) can chicken broth

1 cup half-and-half

salt and pepper to taste

1 pinch ground cinnamon (optional)

DIRECTIONS

1. Melt the butter in a large saucepan over medium-high heat. Sauté the shiitake mushrooms, portobello mushrooms, and shallots for about 5 minutes, or until soft. Mix in the flour until smooth. Gradually stir in the chicken broth. Cook, stirring, 5 minutes, or until thick and bubbly.

2. Stir in the half-and-half, season with salt and pepper, and sprinkle with cinnamon. Heat through, but do not boil.

French Onion Soup VII

Submitted by: **Zabocka**

Makes: 6 servings

Preparation: 10 minutes

Cooking: 30 minutes

Ready In: 40 minutes

"Beautiful French onion soup. Good for a cold evening or after a late night as a midnight snack. Alternatively, grill the bread and cheese first, and serve in soup or on the side. This keeps well; in fact, it gets better with time. Enjoy and experiment!"

INGREDIENTS

¼ cup butter

8 onions, sliced

1 quart vegetable broth

1½ cups white wine

salt and pepper to taste

6 slices baguette

2 cups shredded mozzarella cheese

DIRECTIONS

1. Melt butter in a large pot over medium heat. Sauté onions until deep brown, about 20 minutes. Stir in broth and wine, using a wooden spoon to scrape the bottom of the pot. Season with salt and pepper. Cook until heated through.

2. Preheat oven on broiler setting. Ladle soup into heatproof serving bowls. Top each bowl with a slice of bread, and sprinkle with cheese. Place under a hot broiler until cheese is melted and slightly browned.

Curried Carrot Soup

Submitted by: **Doug Mathews**

Makes: 6 servings

Preparation: 15 minutes

Cooking: 25 minutes

Ready In: 40 minutes

"Quick, easy, and light. Plus it's the only way to get my niece to eat carrots. You can garnish with golden raisins or a dollop of sour cream."

INGREDIENTS

2 tablespoons vegetable oil

1 onion, chopped

1 tablespoon curry powder

2 pounds carrots, chopped

4 cups vegetable broth

2 cups water, or as needed

DIRECTIONS

1. Heat oil in a large pot over medium heat. Sauté onion until tender and translucent. Stir in the curry powder. Add the chopped carrots, and stir until the carrots are coated. Pour in the vegetable broth, and simmer until the carrots are soft, about 20 minutes.

2. Transfer the carrots and broth to a blender, and purée until smooth. Pour back into the pot, and thin with water to your preferred consistency.

Curry Pumpkin Soup

Submitted by: **Mary Ingram**

Makes: 8 servings

Preparation: 5 minutes

Cooking: 15 minutes

Ready In: 20 minutes

"This is a wonderfully soothing and savory soup - a perfect choice for a holiday party or dinner. Adjust the amount of curry and soy sauce for spiciness. Adjust the amount of half-and-half, or substitute heavy cream or milk for varying levels of creaminess. Also, you can add sautéed chopped sweet onions with the first three ingredients (this works best with a creamier version)."

INGREDIENTS

2 tablespoons pumpkin seeds (optional)

2 tablespoons butter

3 tablespoons all-purpose flour

2 tablespoons curry powder

4 cups vegetable broth

1 (29 ounce) can pumpkin

1½ cups half-and-half cream

2 tablespoons soy sauce

1 tablespoon white sugar

salt and pepper to taste

DIRECTIONS

1. Preheat oven to 375 °F (190°C). Arrange pumpkin seeds in a single layer on a baking sheet. Toast in preheated oven for about 10 minutes, or until seeds begin to brown.

2. Melt butter in a large pot over medium heat. Stir in flour and curry powder until smooth. Cook, stirring, until mixture begins to bubble. Gradually whisk in broth, and cook until thickened. Stir in pumpkin and half-and-half. Season with soy sauce, sugar, salt, and pepper. Bring just to a boil, then remove from heat. Garnish with roasted pumpkin seeds.

Curried Cream of Any Veggie Soup

Submitted by: **Dick**

Makes: 6 servings

Preparation: 15 minutes

Cooking: 30 minutes

Ready In: 45 minutes

"A low calorie vegetable soup. Works well with broccoli, mushrooms, potatoes, or celery."

INGREDIENTS

1 tablespoon vegetable oil

1 onion, chopped

1 clove garlic, minced

1 tablespoon curry powder

4 cups chicken broth

4 cups chopped mixed vegetables

2 tablespoons all-purpose flour

2 cups nonfat milk

salt and pepper to taste

DIRECTIONS

1. Heat oil in a large saucepan over medium heat. Sauté onion and garlic until tender. Stir in curry, and cook for 2 minutes, stirring constantly. Add broth and vegetables, and bring to a boil. Simmer 20 minutes, or until tender.

2. Dissolve flour in milk, then stir into the soup. Simmer until thickened. Season with salt and pepper.

Chicken and Dumplings III

Submitted by: **Melissa**

Makes: 6 servings

Preparation: 15 minutes

Cooking: 30 minutes

Ready In: 45 minutes

"My mom used to make this recipe for us growing up. Now I make it for my family and they all love it! It's simple yet delicious! Enjoy!"

INGREDIENTS

6 boneless chicken thighs

2 (10.75 ounce) cans condensed cream of celery soup

salt and pepper to taste

1 (12 ounce) package refrigerated biscuit dough

DIRECTIONS

1. In a large pot over high heat, combine the chicken with enough water to cover, and boil for 15 to 20 minutes. Drain some of the water from the pot, reserving 3 cups in the pot. Remove chicken and allow it to cool, then pull it apart into bite size pieces; return to pot.

2. Reduce heat to medium, and add the cans of condensed soup. Season with salt and pepper. Pull the biscuit dough into pieces, and add to the soup. Simmer over medium heat for 7 to 8 minutes, or until the dough is cooked through.

Grandma's Chicken Noodle Soup

Submitted by: **Corwynn Darkholme**

Makes: 12 servings

Preparation: 20 minutes

Cooking: 25 minutes

Ready In: 45 minutes

"This is a recipe that was given to me by my grandmother. It is a very savory and tasty soup and I believe that all will like it. If you would like to add even more flavor, try using smoked chicken!!"

INGREDIENTS

2¹/₂ cups wide egg noodles

1 teaspoon vegetable oil

12 cups chicken broth

1¹/₂ tablespoons salt

1 teaspoon poultry seasoning

1 cup chopped celery

1 cup chopped onion

¹/₃ cup cornstarch

¹/₄ cup water

3 cups diced, cooked chicken meat

DIRECTIONS

1. Bring a large pot of lightly salted water to a boil. Add egg noodles and oil, and boil for 8 minutes, or until tender. Drain, and rinse under cool running water.

2. In a large saucepan or Dutch oven, combine broth, salt, and poultry seasoning. Bring to a boil. Stir in celery and onion. Reduce heat, cover, and simmer 15 minutes.

3. In a small bowl, mix cornstarch and water together until cornstarch is completely dissolved. Gradually add to soup, stirring constantly. Stir in noodles and chicken, and heat through.

Chicken Tortilla Soup

Submitted by: **Star Pooley**

Makes: 8 servings

Preparation: 20 minutes

Cooking: 20 minutes

Ready In: 40 minutes

"This soup is quick to make, flavorful, and filling! Serve with warm corn bread or tortillas. This also freezes well. Garnish with chopped fresh avocado, Monterey Jack cheese, crushed tortilla chips, or green onion!"

INGREDIENTS

1 onion, chopped

3 cloves garlic, minced

1 tablespoon olive oil

2 teaspoons chili powder

1 teaspoon dried oregano

1 (28 ounce) can crushed tomatoes

1 (10.5 ounce) can condensed chicken broth

1¼ cups water

1 cup whole corn kernels, cooked

1 cup white hominy

1 (4 ounce) can chopped green chile peppers

1 (15 ounce) can black beans, rinsed and drained

¼ cup chopped fresh cilantro

2 boneless chicken breast halves, cooked and cut into bite-sized pieces

crushed tortilla chips

sliced avocado

shredded Monterey Jack cheese

chopped green onions

DIRECTIONS

1. In a medium stock pot, heat oil over medium heat. Sauté onion and garlic in oil until soft. Stir in chili powder, oregano, tomatoes, broth, and water. Bring to a boil, and simmer for 5 to 10 minutes.

2. Stir in corn, hominy, chiles, beans, cilantro, and chicken. Simmer for 10 minutes.

3. Ladle soup into individual serving bowls, and top with crushed tortilla chips, avocado slices, cheese, and chopped green onion.

Six Can Chicken Tortilla Soup

Submitted by: **Terryn**

Makes: 6 servings

Preparation: 5 minutes

Cooking: 15 minutes

Ready In: 20 minutes

"Delicious and EASY zesty soup recipe that uses only 6 canned ingredients! Serve over tortilla chips, and top with shredded Cheddar cheese. Throw away the cans and no one will know that it is not from scratch!"

INGREDIENTS

1 (15 ounce) can whole kernel corn, drained

2 (14.5 ounce) cans chicken broth

1 (10 ounce) can chunk chicken

1 (15 ounce) can black beans

1 (10 ounce) can diced tomatoes with green chile peppers, drained

DIRECTIONS

1. Open the cans of corn, chicken broth, chunk chicken, black beans, and diced tomatoes with green chilies. Pour everything into a large saucepan or stock pot. Simmer over medium heat until chicken is heated through.

Patricia's Green Chile Soup

Submitted by: **Patricia Collins**

Makes: 4 servings

Preparation: 5 minutes

Cooking: 20 minutes

Ready In: 25 minutes

"This is an easy, hearty, spicy soup. I have found that it is a favorite even with picky people! The recipe is always requested. Serve with warm buttered tortillas, cheese, and sour cream."

INGREDIENTS

1 tablespoon butter

1/2 cup finely diced onion

1 teaspoon minced garlic

1/2 cup chopped fresh green chile peppers

1 (5 ounce) can chunk chicken

1 1/2 teaspoons ground cumin

1 (10.75 ounce) can condensed cream of chicken soup

1 1/4 cups half-and-half cream

1 cup shredded Cheddar cheese

1/4 cup sour cream

DIRECTIONS

1. Melt butter in a large saucepan over medium-high heat. Sauté onion until transparent. Stir in the garlic, green chiles, chicken meat, and cumin. Cook for one minute to blend the flavors. Stir in the cream of chicken soup and half-and-half. Cook until heated through, about 5 minutes. Ladle hot soup into bowls. Top with cheese and a dollop of sour cream.

Southwestern Turkey Soup

Submitted by: **Doug Matthews**

Makes: 8 servings

Preparation: 15 minutes

Cooking: 30 minutes

Ready In: 45 minutes

"An interesting solution to the leftover Thanksgiving turkey dilemma. My 2 1/2 year old daughter helped me make it this year. I like to serve it with warm corn bread."

INGREDIENTS

1½ cups shredded cooked turkey

4 cups vegetable broth

1 (28 ounce) can whole peeled tomatoes

1 (4 ounce) can chopped green chile peppers

2 roma (plum) tomatoes, chopped

1 onion, chopped

2 cloves garlic, crushed

1 tablespoon lime juice

½ teaspoon cayenne pepper

½ teaspoon ground cumin

salt and pepper to taste

1 avocado - peeled, pitted and diced

½ teaspoon dried cilantro

1 cup shredded Monterey Jack cheese

DIRECTIONS

1. In a large pot over medium heat, combine turkey, broth, canned tomatoes, green chiles, fresh tomatoes, onion, garlic, and lime juice. Season with cayenne, cumin, salt, and pepper. Bring to a boil, then reduce heat, and simmer 15 to 20 minutes.

2. Stir in avocado and cilantro, and simmer 15 to 20 minutes, until slightly thickened. Spoon into serving bowls, and top with shredded cheese.

White Chili

Submitted by: **Dierdre Dee**

Makes: 4 servings

Preparation: 10 minutes

Cooking: 25 minutes

Ready In: 35 minutes

"Serve with corn bread and salad. If you cube the chicken ahead of time, make corn bread muffins while preparing the chili, and use a bagged salad mix from the produce department, this is a very fast meal to put together."

INGREDIENTS

1 tablespoon olive oil

1 pound skinless, boneless chicken breast halves - cubed

1 onion, chopped

1¼ cups chicken broth

1 (4 ounce) can diced green chiles

1 teaspoon garlic powder

1 teaspoon ground cumin

½ teaspoon dried oregano

½ teaspoon dried cilantro

⅛ teaspoon cayenne pepper

1 (15 ounce) can cannellini beans, drained and rinsed

2 green onions, chopped

2 ounces shredded Monterey Jack cheese

DIRECTIONS

1. Heat oil in a large saucepan over medium-high heat. Cook chicken and onion in oil 4 to 5 minutes, or until onion is tender.

2. Stir in the chicken broth, green chiles, garlic powder, cumin, oregano, cilantro, and cayenne pepper. Reduce heat, and simmer for 15 minutes.

3. Stir in the beans, and simmer for 5 more minutes, or until chicken is no longer pink and juices run clear. Garnish with green onion and shredded cheese.

Taco Soup

Submitted by: **Darla Williams**

Makes: 6 servings

Preparation: 5 minutes

Cooking: 25 minutes

Ready In: 30 minutes

"Like a taco in a bowl! Serve with cheese, tortilla chips, and sour cream."

INGREDIENTS

½ pound ground beef

¼ cup chopped onion

1½ cups water

1 (16 ounce) can chopped stewed tomatoes, with juice

1 (15 ounce) can kidney beans with liquid

1 (8 ounce) can tomato sauce

2 tablespoons taco seasoning mix

1 avocado - peeled, pitted and diced

1 cup shredded Cheddar cheese (optional)

1 (12 ounce) package corn tortilla chips (optional)

1 (8 ounce) container sour cream (optional)

DIRECTIONS

1. In a large saucepan over medium heat, cook ground beef and onion until meat is evenly brown; drain excess fat. Mix in water, tomatoes, kidney beans, tomato sauce, and taco seasoning mix. Cover, and simmer for 15 minutes. Remove from heat, and stir in the avocado.

2. Ladle hot soup into serving bowls. Pass cheese, tortilla chips, and sour cream to top each serving.

Miso Soup

Submitted by: **Michelle Chen**

Makes: 4 servings

Preparation: 5 minutes

Cooking: 15 minutes

Ready In: 20 minutes

"Dashi is a basic stock used in Japanese cooking which is made by boiling dried kelp (seaweed) and dried bonito (fish). Instant dashi granules are sold in conveniently-sized jars or packets and vary in strength. Add more dashi to your soup if you want a stronger stock. You can use yellow, white or red miso paste for this soup. Yellow miso is sweet and creamy, red miso is stronger and saltier."

INGREDIENTS

2 teaspoons dashi granules

4 cups water

3 tablespoons miso paste

1 (8 ounce) package silken tofu, diced

2 green onions, sliced diagonally into ½ inch pieces

DIRECTIONS

1. In a medium saucepan over medium-high heat, combine dashi granules and water; bring to a boil. Reduce heat to medium, and whisk in the miso paste. Stir in tofu. Separate the layers of the green onions, and add them to the soup. Simmer gently for 2 to 3 minutes before serving.

Vegan Black Bean Soup

Submitted by: **Christine**

Makes: 6 servings

Preparation: 15 minutes

Cooking: 30 minutes

Ready In: 45 minutes

"Easy to make, thick, hearty soup with a zesty flavor."

INGREDIENTS

1 tablespoon olive oil

1 large onion, chopped

1 stalk celery, chopped

2 carrots, chopped

4 cloves garlic, chopped

2 tablespoons chili powder

1 tablespoon ground cumin

1 pinch black pepper

4 cups vegetable broth

4 (15 ounce) cans black beans

1 (15 ounce) can whole kernel corn

1 (14.5 ounce) can crushed tomatoes

DIRECTIONS

1. Heat oil in a large pot over medium-high heat. Sauté onion, celery, carrots and garlic for 5 minutes. Season with chili powder, cumin, and black pepper; cook for 1 minute. Stir in vegetable broth, 2 cans of beans, and corn. Bring to a boil.

2. Meanwhile, in a food processor or blender, process remaining 2 cans beans and tomatoes until smooth. Stir into boiling soup mixture, reduce heat to medium, and simmer for 15 minutes.

Insanely Easy Vegetarian Chili

Submitted by: **Tianne**

Makes: 8 servings
Preparation: 25 minutes
Cooking: 30 minutes
Ready In: 55 minutes

"This chili is SO easy to make. You can pretty much throw whatever you have into the pot and it'll be great. (I added some leftover salsa once.) It's very colorful, not to mention delicious."

INGREDIENTS

1 tablespoon vegetable oil

1 cup chopped onions

³/4 cup chopped carrots

3 cloves garlic, minced

1 cup chopped green bell pepper

1 cup chopped red bell pepper

³/4 cup chopped celery

1 tablespoon chili powder

1¹/2 cups chopped fresh mushrooms

1 (28 ounce) can whole peeled tomatoes with liquid, chopped

1 (19 ounce) can kidney beans with liquid

1 (11 ounce) can whole kernel corn, undrained

1 tablespoon ground cumin

1¹/2 teaspoons oregano

1¹/2 teaspoons dried basil

DIRECTIONS

1. Heat oil in a large saucepan over medium heat. Sauté onions, carrots, and garlic until tender. Stir in green pepper, red pepper, celery, and chili powder. Cook until vegetables are tender, about 6 minutes.

2. Stir in mushrooms, and cook 4 minutes. Stir in tomatoes, kidney beans, and corn. Season with cumin, oregano, and basil. Bring to a boil, and reduce heat to medium. Cover, and simmer for 20 minutes, stirring occasionally.

Big Ed's Cajun Shrimp Soup

Submitted by: **Eddie**

Makes: 6 servings

Preparation: 15 minutes

Cooking: 25 minutes

Ready In: 40 minutes

"This is an excellent recipe that is quick and easy to fix, and it tastes great too!"

INGREDIENTS

1 tablespoon butter

1/2 cup chopped green bell pepper

1/4 cup sliced green onions

1 clove garlic, minced

3 cups tomato-vegetable juice cocktail

1 (8 ounce) bottle clam juice

1/2 cup water

1/4 teaspoon dried thyme

1/4 teaspoon dried basil

1/4 teaspoon red pepper flakes

1 bay leaf

1/2 teaspoon salt

1/2 cup uncooked long-grain white rice

3/4 pound fresh shrimp, peeled and deveined

hot pepper sauce to taste

DIRECTIONS

1. Melt butter in a large pot over medium heat. Sauté green bell pepper, onions, and garlic until tender. Stir in vegetable juice, clam juice, and water. Season with thyme, basil, red pepper, bay leaf, and salt. Bring to a boil, and stir in rice. Reduce heat, and cover. Simmer 15 minutes, until rice is tender.

2. Stir in shrimp, and cook 5 minutes, or until shrimp are opaque. Remove the bay leaf, and season with hot sauce.

Cajun Crab Soup

Submitted by: **Doreen**

Makes: 8 servings

Preparation: 15 minutes

Cooking: 30 minutes

Ready In: 45 minutes

"This rich, delicious soup is modeled after a great soup that we had in a restaurant in Bethany Beach, Delaware!"

INGREDIENTS

½ cup unsalted butter

1 onion, chopped

2 cloves garlic, minced

¼ cup all-purpose flour

2 cups clam juice

2 cups chicken broth

1 (10 ounce) package frozen white corn

1 teaspoon salt

½ teaspoon ground white pepper

¼ teaspoon dried thyme

¼ teaspoon ground cayenne pepper

2 cups heavy cream

1 pound lump crabmeat, drained

4 green onions, chopped

DIRECTIONS

1. Melt butter in a large saucepan over medium heat. Sauté onion and garlic until onion is tender. Whisk in flour, and cook 2 minutes. Stir in clam juice and chicken broth, and bring to a boil. Mix in corn, and season with salt, white pepper, thyme, and cayenne. Reduce heat, and simmer 15 minutes.

2. Stir in cream, crab meat, and green onions. Heat through, but do not boil once the cream has been added.

Awesome Crab Soup

Submitted by: **Yvette Martell**

Makes: 4 servings

Preparation: 10 minutes

Cooking: 20 minutes

Ready In: 30 minutes

"Creamy crab soup at its best. I can honestly say that this is perfect."

INGREDIENTS

½ cup butter

⅓ cup all-purpose flour

1 teaspoon Old Bay® Seasoning

1 tablespoon Worcestershire sauce

1 (14.5 ounce) can chicken broth

1 cup dry white wine

1 cup half-and-half cream

1 (2.5 ounce) package country style gravy mix

8 ounces crabmeat

4 drops hot sauce

½ teaspoon salt

½ teaspoon ground black pepper

DIRECTIONS

1. Melt butter in a large saucepan over low heat. Stir in flour all at once, and cook until bubbly. Stir in Old Bay seasoning and Worcestershire sauce. Gradually stir in chicken broth, wine, and half-and-half.

2. Prepare gravy according to package directions, and stir into soup. Thin with more half-and-half if necessary. Simmer 10 minutes, stirring occasionally.

3. Stir in crabmeat, and season with hot sauce, salt, and pepper. Simmer 2 minutes, or until heated through.

Crawfish Chowder

Submitted by: **Tina**

Makes: 10 servings
Preparation: 20 minutes
Cooking: 25 minutes
Ready In: 45 minutes

"I serve this chowder Christmas night. Everyone welcomes the change from all of the junk food and turkey. It is very creamy and satisfying. Serve it with corn bread or crusty French bread."

INGREDIENTS

¼ cup butter

½ bunch green onions, chopped

½ cup butter

2 pounds frozen crawfish, cleaned

2 (10.75 ounce) cans condensed cream of potato soup

1 (10.75 ounce) can condensed cream of mushroom soup

1 (15.25 ounce) can whole kernel corn, drained

4 ounces cream cheese, softened

2 cups half-and-half cream

½ teaspoon cayenne pepper

DIRECTIONS

1. Melt ¼ cup of butter in a large skillet over medium heat. Sauté green onions in butter until tender. Remove from pan, and set aside. In the same skillet, melt ½ cup of butter, and sauté the crawfish for 5 minutes; set aside.

2. In a large pot over medium heat, combine potato soup, mushroom soup, corn, and cream cheese. Mix well, and bring to a slow boil. Stir in half-and-half, sautéed green onions, and crawfish. Season with cayenne pepper. Bring to a low boil, and simmer 5 minutes to blend flavors.

New England Clam Chowder

Submitted by: **Debbie Orem**

Makes: 8 servings

Preparation: 15 minutes

Cooking: 30 minutes

Ready In: 45 minutes

"Hot and hearty recipe that will warm you up on cold winter days."

INGREDIENTS

4 slices bacon, diced

1½ cups chopped onion

1½ cups water

4 cups peeled and cubed potatoes

1½ teaspoons salt

ground black pepper to taste

3 cups half-and-half

3 tablespoons butter

2 (10 ounce) cans minced clams

DIRECTIONS

1. Place diced bacon in large stock pot over medium-high heat. Cook until almost crisp; add onions, and cook 5 minutes. Stir in water and potatoes, and season with salt and pepper. Bring to a boil, and cook uncovered for 15 minutes, or until potatoes are fork tender.

2. Pour in half-and-half, and add butter. Drain clams, reserving clam liquid; stir clams and ½ of the clam liquid into the soup. Cook for about 5 minutes, or until heated through. Do not allow to boil.

Salmon Chowder

Submitted by: **Kenulia**

Makes: 8 servings

Preparation: 15 minutes

Cooking: 30 minutes

Ready In: 45 minutes

"I don't like fish, but I LOVE this soup!"

INGREDIENTS

3 tablespoons butter

3/4 cup chopped onion

1/2 cup chopped celery

1 teaspoon garlic powder

2 cups diced potatoes

2 carrots, diced

2 cups chicken broth

1 teaspoon salt

1 teaspoon ground black pepper

1 teaspoon dried dill weed

2 (16 ounce) cans salmon

1 (12 fluid ounce) can evaporated milk

1 (15 ounce) can creamed corn

1/2 pound Cheddar cheese, shredded

DIRECTIONS

1. Melt butter in a large pot over medium heat. Sauté onion, celery, and garlic powder until onions are tender. Stir in potatoes, carrots, broth, salt, pepper, and dill. Bring to a boil, and reduce heat. Cover, and simmer 20 minutes.

2. Stir in salmon, evaporated milk, corn, and cheese. Cook until heated through.

pasta

Pasta is the ultimate fast food: Boil it for ten minutes while you make the sauce, and dinner is ready before the "I'm hungry!" chorus has time to warm up. Your choices in the pasta aisle are forever expanding; have some fun with all the different shapes and colors available now. Sample the fresh or frozen ravioli and tortellini. Try the imported pasta labeled 'durum wheat' or 'semolina' and let their superior texture and flavor be the star. 'Plain old spaghetti' will never be boring again.

Asparagus, Chicken and Penne Pasta

Submitted by: **Jessie**

Makes: 8 servings

Preparation: 15 minutes

Cooking: 20 minutes

Ready In: 35 minutes

"This dish is slightly spicy. It has a unique and awesome taste!"

INGREDIENTS

1 (16 ounce) package dry penne pasta

2 tablespoons olive oil, divided

3/4 pound skinless, boneless chicken breast halves - cut into bite size pieces

4 cloves garlic, minced

12 ounces asparagus, trimmed and cut into 1 inch pieces

1 teaspoon crushed red pepper flakes

salt and pepper to taste

1/2 cup grated Parmesan cheese

DIRECTIONS

1. Bring a large pot of lightly salted water to a boil. Cook pasta in boiling water for 8 to 10 minutes, or until al dente. Drain, and transfer to a large bowl.

2. Heat 1 tablespoon olive oil in a large skillet over medium heat. Sauté chicken until firm and lightly browned; remove from pan. Add the remaining tablespoon of olive oil to the skillet. Cook and stir garlic, asparagus, and red pepper flakes in oil until asparagus is tender. Stir in chicken, and cook for 2 minutes to blend the flavors. Season with salt and pepper.

3. Toss pasta with chicken and asparagus mixture. Sprinkle with Parmesan cheese.

Chicken and Asparagus Fettuccine

Submitted by: **Stephanie Moon**

Makes: 6 servings

Preparation: 15 minutes

Cooking: 25 minutes

Ready In: 40 minutes

"This is so rich and filling that one serving goes a long way. Crusty bread and a salad is all this creamy dish needs to make a complete and hearty meal."

INGREDIENTS

12 ounces dry fettuccine pasta

2 cups 1 inch pieces fresh asparagus

1/2 cup butter

2 cups half-and-half cream

1/4 teaspoon garlic powder

1/4 teaspoon ground black pepper

1 pinch cayenne pepper

3/4 cup grated Parmesan cheese

1/2 pound cooked chicken breasts - cut into bite size pieces

DIRECTIONS

1. Bring a large pot of lightly salted water to a boil. Add pasta, and cook for 8 to 10 minutes, or until al dente. Add the asparagus during the last 3 to 5 minutes of cooking. Drain, and transfer to a large bowl.

2. In a large saucepan over medium heat, combine butter and half-and-half. Cook until thick and bubbly. Season with garlic powder, black pepper, and cayenne pepper. Stir in Parmesan cheese and chicken, and heat through.

3. Pour sauce over pasta and asparagus, and toss to coat.

Chicken Alfredo

Submitted by: **Lisa B.**

Makes: 4 servings

Preparation: 20 minutes

Cooking: 20 minutes

Ready In: 40 minutes

"Quick and easy dinner with broccoli, zucchini, and red bell pepper. The sauce is enriched by cream cheese."

INGREDIENTS

6 ounces dry fettuccine pasta

1 (8 ounce) package cream cheese

6 tablespoons butter

½ cup milk

½ teaspoon garlic powder

salt and pepper to taste

2 boneless skinless chicken breasts, cooked and cubed

2 cups chopped fresh broccoli

2 small zucchini, julienned

½ cup chopped red bell pepper

DIRECTIONS

1. Bring a large pot of lightly salted water to a boil. Add pasta, and cook for 8 to 10 minutes, or until al dente; drain.

2. While pasta is cooking, melt cream cheese and butter in a skillet over low heat. Stir until smooth. Stir in milk, and season with garlic powder, salt, and pepper. Simmer for 3 minutes, or until thickened, stirring constantly.

3. Mix in chicken, broccoli, zucchini, and red pepper. Cook 3 minutes over medium heat, then reduce heat, and simmer 5 minutes, or until vegetables are tender. Serve over fettuccine.

Easy Chicken Alfredo II

Submitted by: **Sara**

Makes: 4 servings

Preparation: 15 minutes

Cooking: 15 minutes

Ready In: 30 minutes

"Leftover chicken breast in a cottage cheese sauce, served on a bed of fettuccine pasta."

INGREDIENTS

8 ounces dry fettuccine pasta

1 cup milk

2 tablespoons all-purpose flour

1 cup cottage cheese

1/2 teaspoon garlic powder

3 teaspoons minced onion

salt and pepper to taste

1/2 cup grated Parmesan cheese

2 cups diced, cooked chicken breast meat

DIRECTIONS

1. Bring a large pot of lightly salted water to a boil. Cook pasta in boiling water for 8 to 10 minutes, or until al dente; drain, and set aside.

2. In a food processor, place the milk, flour, cottage cheese, garlic powder, onion, salt and pepper, and Parmesan cheese. Blend until smooth.

3. Transfer the blended mixture to a saucepan over medium heat. Mix in the chicken, and cook until heated through. Serve hot over pasta.

Chicken Rotini Stovetop Casserole

Submitted by: **Terry**

Makes: 6 servings

Preparation: 15 minutes

Cooking: 25 minutes

Ready In: 40 minutes

"Rotini pasta tossed with chicken, bell pepper and a creamy herb sauce - all prepared on the stovetop! Very quick and easy recipe. You can improvise to certain tastes, and serve it for any occasion."

INGREDIENTS

1 (12 ounce) package rotini pasta

2 cups half-and-half cream

1/2 cup butter

2/3 cup freshly grated Parmesan cheese

1/2 teaspoon dried basil leaves

1/2 teaspoon dried oregano

1/2 teaspoon chopped fresh chives

1/2 teaspoon chopped fresh parsley

4 skinless, boneless chicken breast halves - cubed

1/2 green bell pepper, chopped

1/2 red bell pepper, chopped

DIRECTIONS

1. Bring a large pot of lightly salted water to a boil. Add pasta, and cook for 8 to 10 minutes, or until al dente; drain.

2. Combine half-and-half and butter in a saucepan over medium heat. Boil gently, stirring, until mixture has reduced to 1½ to 1⅔ cups. Remove pan from heat; whisk in cheese, basil, oregano, chives, and parsley. Cover, and set aside.

3. Sauté chicken in a large skillet until lightly browned on both sides. Stir in green and red bell pepper, and cook until vegetables are tender, and chicken is no longer pink in the middle.

4. In a casserole dish, combine the hot cooked pasta, chicken mixture, and sauce. Mix well, and serve immediately.

Incredibly Easy Chicken and Noodles

Submitted by: **Tammy Christie**

Makes: 6 servings

Preparation: 10 minutes

Cooking: 30 minutes

Ready In: 40 minutes

"My aunt gave me this recipe. She is known for her chicken and noodles, and everyone thinks she makes them from scratch. This recipe is very easy and fast."

INGREDIENTS

1 (26 ounce) can condensed cream of chicken soup

1 (10.75 ounce) can condensed cream of mushroom soup

3 (14.5 ounce) cans chicken broth

2 cups diced, cooked chicken breast meat

2 teaspoons onion powder

1 teaspoon seasoning salt

1/2 teaspoon garlic powder

2 (9 ounce) packages frozen egg noodles

DIRECTIONS

1. In a large pot, mix the cream of chicken soup, cream of mushroom soup, chicken broth, and chicken meat. Season with onion powder, seasoning salt, and garlic powder. Bring to a boil, and stir in the noodles. Reduce heat to low, and simmer for 20 to 30 minutes.

Pasta with Kielbasa and Sauerkraut

Submitted by: **Gail**

Makes: 6 servings

Preparation: 20 minutes

Cooking: 20 minutes

Ready In: 40 minutes

"Fast, easy and something a little different."

INGREDIENTS

12 ounces dry ziti pasta

3 tablespoons olive oil

1 onion, chopped

1 red bell pepper, chopped

2 cloves garlic, minced

1 pound kielbasa sausage, sliced into
½ inch pieces

12 ounces sauerkraut, drained and rinsed

2 tablespoons prepared Dijon-style mustard

1 pinch cayenne pepper

¼ cup white wine

2 tablespoons chopped fresh parsley

DIRECTIONS

1. Bring a large pot of lightly salted water to a boil. Add pasta, and cook for 8 to 10 minutes, or until al dente; drain.

2. Heat olive oil in a large skillet over medium heat. Cook onion and bell pepper in oil, stirring frequently, until onion is tender. Stir in garlic and kielbasa, and cook until kielbasa begins to brown, about 8 minutes. Stir in sauerkraut, mustard, and cayenne; cook about 4 minutes more. Stir in wine and parsley, and heat through.

3. Toss ziti with kielbasa and sauerkraut, and serve immediately.

Bow Ties with Sausage, Tomatoes and Cream

Submitted by: **Linda Caroline**

Makes: 6 servings

Preparation: 15 minutes

Cooking: 30 minutes

Ready In: 45 minutes

"A friend gave this recipe to me a few years back, and my family can't seem to get enough of it. It sounds strange with cream in it, but that just enhances the flavor and texture. This is a very easy recipe."

INGREDIENTS

1 (12 ounce) package bow tie pasta

2 tablespoons olive oil

1 pound sweet Italian sausage, casings removed and crumbled

1/2 teaspoon red pepper flakes

1/2 cup diced onion

3 cloves garlic, minced

1 (28 ounce) can Italian-style plum tomatoes, drained and coarsely chopped

1 1/2 cups heavy cream

1/2 teaspoon salt

3 tablespoons minced fresh parsley

DIRECTIONS

1. Bring a large pot of lightly salted water to a boil. Cook pasta in boiling water for 8 to 10 minutes, or until al dente; drain.

2. Heat oil in a large, deep skillet over medium heat. Cook sausage and pepper flakes until sausage is evenly brown. Stir in onion and garlic, and cook until onion is tender. Stir in tomatoes, cream, and salt. Simmer until mixture thickens, 8 to 10 minutes.

3. Stir cooked pasta into sauce, and heat through. Sprinkle with parsley.

Leftover Special Casserole

Submitted by: **Lenna Roe**

Makes: 6 servings

Preparation: 15 minutes

Cooking: 30 minutes

Ready In: 45 minutes

"This kind of came together after a holiday dinner that left lots of ingredients left over. You can also use leftover chicken, beef or turkey for the meat."

INGREDIENTS

4 cups uncooked egg noodles

1 (10 ounce) package frozen mixed peas and carrots, thawed

1 small onion, minced

2 cups cooked ham, diced

1 (10.75 ounce) can condensed cream of mushroom soup

½ cup milk

salt and pepper to taste

DIRECTIONS

1. Preheat oven to 350°F (175°C). Lightly grease a 9x13 inch baking dish. Bring a large pot of water to a boil. Add egg noodles, and cook for 8 to 10 minutes, or until done; drain.

2. Layer noodles, mixed peas and carrots, onions, and ham in prepared baking dish. Mix together soup and milk, then pour mixture over casserole. Season with salt and pepper, then press with the back of a fork to help soup mixture seep through casserole layers.

3. Bake at 350°F (175°C) for 30 minutes, or until bubbly and hot.

Angel Hair Pasta with Shrimp and Basil

Makes: 4 servings
Preparation: 10 minutes
Cooking: 25 minutes
Ready In: 35 minutes

Submitted by: **Pat Lowe**

"If you like the ingredients in the name, you'll love the dish. Freshly grated Parmesan cheese makes it complete."

INGREDIENTS

1/4 cup olive oil, divided

1 (8 ounce) package angel hair pasta

1 teaspoon chopped garlic

1 pound large shrimp - peeled and deveined

2 (28 ounce) cans Italian-style diced tomatoes, drained

1/2 cup dry white wine

1/4 cup chopped parsley

3 tablespoons chopped fresh basil

3 tablespoons freshly grated Parmesan cheese

DIRECTIONS

1. Bring a large pot of water to a boil, and add 1 tablespoon oil. Cook pasta in boiling water until al dente. Place pasta in a colander, and give it a quick rinse with cold water.

2. Heat remaining olive oil in a 10 inch skillet over medium heat. Cook garlic, stirring constantly, until the garlic is tender, about 1 minute. Do not let the garlic burn. Add shrimp, and cook for 3 to 5 minutes. Remove shrimp from the skillet, and set aside.

3. Stir tomatoes, wine, parsley, and basil into the skillet. Continue cooking, stirring occasionally, until liquid is reduced by half, 8 to 12 minutes. Add shrimp, and continue cooking until the shrimp are heated through, about 2 to 3 minutes. Serve the shrimp mixture over the pasta. Sprinkle with Parmesan cheese.

Lemon Pepper Pasta Seafood

Submitted by: **Catherine Neal**

Makes: 4 servings

Preparation: 20 minutes

Cooking: 10 minutes

Ready In: 30 minutes

"Lemon pepper pasta served with sautéed garlic seafood. You can substitute the shrimp in this recipe with crab or scallops, or you could use a mixture of all three types of seafood."

INGREDIENTS

1 (8 ounce) package lemon pepper linguine

4 tablespoons olive oil

2 tablespoons chopped garlic

1 tablespoon lemon pepper

1 pound medium shrimp - peeled and deveined

½ cup grated Parmesan cheese

DIRECTIONS

1. Bring a large pot of lightly salted water to boil, add pasta, and cook for 8 to 10 minutes, or until al dente. Drain, and return pasta to the pot.

2. Heat olive oil in a skillet over medium heat. Cook garlic, lemon pepper seasoning, and shrimp in oil until shrimp is cooked through, 3 to 5 minutes.

3. Toss pasta with shrimp and Parmesan cheese.

Shrimp Linguine

Submitted by: **Jessica**

Makes: 6 servings

Preparation: 20 minutes

Cooking: 20 minutes

Ready In: 40 minutes

"I created this dish after trying a similar dish (made with crab) at a restaurant. It's wonderful! If you like, you can garnish with additional chopped tomato and chopped green onion. If you have the time, toasting the pine nuts will enhance the flavor."

INGREDIENTS

1 (12 ounce) package linguine pasta

1/4 pound bacon

2 tablespoons olive oil

3 cloves garlic, minced

2 tablespoons chopped fresh oregano

2 tablespoons chopped fresh basil

3 roma (plum) tomatoes, seeded and chopped

1/2 cup chopped green onions

1 cup half-and-half cream

1/4 cup freshly grated Parmesan cheese

1/4 cup shredded Monterey Jack cheese

1 pound cooked shrimp

1/4 cup toasted pine nuts (optional)

DIRECTIONS

1. Bring a large pot of lightly salted water to a boil. Cook pasta in boiling water for 8 to 10 minutes, or until al dente; drain.

2. Place bacon in a large, deep skillet. Cook over medium-high heat until evenly brown. Drain, crumble, and set aside.

3. Heat olive oil in a large skillet over medium heat. Sauté garlic, basil, and oregano in oil for 1 minute. Stir in tomatoes and green onions, and sauté for 3 minutes. Add bacon, half and half, Parmesan cheese, and Monterey Jack cheese. Cook until cheese is just melted. Stir in shrimp, and cook until heated through, about 2 minutes.

4. Serve sauce over pasta, and sprinkle with pine nuts.

Seafood Piccata

Submitted by: **Beth Lewis**

Makes: 8 servings

Preparation: 35 minutes

Cooking: 20 minutes

Ready In: 55 minutes

"Shrimp, scallops and crabmeat sautéed in a white wine and lemon sauce and tossed with hot cooked pasta shells. Every time I cook for a large group, this is requested. Great tasting and really simple to make!"

INGREDIENTS

1 (16 ounce) package medium shell pasta

6 tablespoons olive oil

1 cup fresh mushrooms, sliced

3/4 cup minced green onions

2 tablespoons minced garlic

1 pound medium shrimp - peeled and deveined

1 pound bay scallops

1 pound crabmeat

2 cups dry white wine

6 tablespoons fresh lemon juice

1/2 cup butter

1/4 cup chopped fresh parsley

DIRECTIONS

1. Bring a large pot of lightly salted water to boil, add pasta shells, and cook for 8 to 10 minutes, or until al dente; drain.

2. Heat olive oil in a large pot over medium heat. Sauté mushrooms, green onions, and garlic until tender. Stir in shrimp, scallops, and crabmeat. Cook for 5 minutes, or until shrimp is pink. Stir in wine, lemon juice, and butter; cook until heated through.

3. Toss pasta with seafood sauce and parsley.

Fra Diavolo Sauce With Pasta

Submitted by: **Holly**

Makes: 8 servings

Preparation: 20 minutes

Cooking: 40 minutes

Ready In: 1 hour

"This sauce includes shrimp and scallops, best served with linguine pasta."

INGREDIENTS

4 tablespoons olive oil, divided

6 cloves garlic, crushed

3 cups whole peeled tomatoes with liquid, chopped

1 1/2 teaspoons salt

1 teaspoon crushed red pepper flakes

1 (16 ounce) package linguine pasta

8 ounces small shrimp, peeled and deveined

8 ounces bay scallops

1 tablespoon chopped fresh parsley

DIRECTIONS

1. In a large saucepan, heat 2 tablespoons of the olive oil with the garlic over medium heat. When the garlic starts to sizzle, pour in the tomatoes. Season with salt and red pepper. Bring to a boil. Lower the heat, and simmer for 30 minutes, stirring occasionally.

2. Meanwhile, bring a large pot of lightly salted water to a boil. Cook pasta for 8 to 10 minutes, or until al dente; drain.

3. In a large skillet, heat the remaining 2 tablespoons of olive oil over high heat. Add the shrimp and scallops. Cook for about 2 minutes, stirring frequently, or until the shrimp turn pink. Add shrimp and scallops to the tomato mixture, and stir in the parsley. Cook for 3 to 4 minutes, or until the sauce just begins to bubble. Serve sauce over pasta.

Scrumptious Seafood Linguine

Submitted by: **Jenni Lawson**

Makes: 6 servings

Preparation: 15 minutes

Cooking: 15 minutes

Ready In: 30 minutes

"If you love seafood and pasta, you will love this dish! It is so easy to make that I make it at least once a month."

INGREDIENTS

2 (9 ounce) packages fresh linguine pasta

1/4 cup butter

1 clove garlic, chopped

1 cup heavy cream

1/2 pound imitation crabmeat

1/2 pound cooked salad shrimp

1 cup freshly grated Parmesan cheese

salt and pepper to taste

1 tablespoon chopped fresh parsley

DIRECTIONS

1. Bring a large pot of lightly salted water to a boil. Add pasta, and cook for 3 minutes, or until al dente; drain.

2. Melt butter in a large skillet over medium heat. Sauté garlic until tender. Stir in cream, and cook until thickened, about 5 minutes. Add imitation crab, shrimp, Parmesan cheese, and salt and pepper. Reduce heat to low, and cook for 2 to 3 minutes, until heated through.

3. Transfer cooked linguine to a serving platter, and top with seafood sauce. Garnish with parsley.

Crawfish Linguine

Submitted by: **Jacqueline**

Makes: 4 servings

Preparation: 10 minutes

Cooking: 15 minutes

Ready In: 25 minutes

"I am married, have a daughter, and work full-time outside the home. Nutritious, quick and simple is my game. This is a simple meal that can be prepared in 25 minutes that is absolutely delicious. Serve with a salad and garlic bread for a complete meal."

INGREDIENTS

1 (8 ounce) package linguine pasta

1/2 cup butter

1/4 cup olive oil

1 clove garlic, crushed

1 cup sliced mushrooms

1 pound crawfish tails

1/2 cup chopped green onions

1 cup half-and-half cream

1/3 cup grated Parmesan cheese

1/4 cup chopped fresh parsley

salt and pepper to taste

DIRECTIONS

1. Bring a large pot of lightly salted water to a boil. Cook pasta for 8 to 10 minutes, or until al dente; drain.

2. Melt butter with olive oil in a large skillet over medium heat. Sauté garlic and mushrooms until tender. Stir in crawfish and green onions; reduce heat to low, and cook 5 minutes. Stir in half and half, Parmesan cheese, and parsley. Simmer for 5 minutes. Season with salt and pepper, and serve over hot linguine.

One Pot Tuna Casserole

Submitted by: **Mary**

Makes: 8 servings

Preparation: 10 minutes

Cooking: 20 minutes

Ready In: 30 minutes

"This is so easy and fast, like tuna casserole without baking it!"

INGREDIENTS

1 (16 ounce) package egg noodles

1 (10 ounce) package frozen green peas, thawed

¼ cup butter

1 (10.75 ounce) can condensed cream of mushroom soup

1 (6 ounce) can tuna, drained

¼ cup milk

1 cup shredded Cheddar cheese

DIRECTIONS

1. Bring a large pot of lightly salted water to a boil. Cook pasta in boiling water until al dente, adding peas for the final 3 minutes of cooking; drain.

2. Melt the butter in the same pot over medium heat. Add the mushroom soup, tuna, milk, and Cheddar cheese. Stir until cheese is melted, and the mixture is smooth. Stir in the pasta and peas until evenly coated.

Tuna Noodle Casserole IV

Submitted by: **Richard**

Makes: 4 servings

Preparation: 20 minutes

Cooking: 30 minutes

Ready In: 50 minutes

"Tuna Macaroni Casserole. It's quick and easy, but the BEST. It will serve the heartiest of family appetites, or a gourmet party."

INGREDIENTS

2 cups elbow macaroni

1 (9 ounce) can tuna, drained

1 (10.75 ounce) can condensed cream of mushroom soup

1 (10.75 ounce) can milk

1 cup shredded sharp Cheddar cheese

1 cup crushed croutons

DIRECTIONS

1. Preheat oven to 350°F (175°C).

2. Bring a large pot of lightly salted water to a boil. Cook macaroni in boiling water for 8 to 10 minutes, or until al dente; drain.

3. In a medium bowl, combine tuna, condensed soup, and milk. Mix with the macaroni, and pour into 2 quart casserole dish. Sprinkle Cheddar cheese and crushed croutons over top.

4. Bake in a preheated oven for 20 to 30 minutes, or until bubbling and browned on the top.

Cheese Ravioli with Three Pepper Topping

Submitted by: **Amanda**

Makes: 6 servings

Preparation: 15 minutes

Cooking: 20 minutes

Ready In: 35 minutes

"A nice change from tomato sauces. I cooked this one day for myself, and my family ate all of it before I had a chance. It's that good."

INGREDIENTS

1 pound cheese ravioli

3 tablespoons olive oil

1 small onion, diced

1 green bell pepper, thinly sliced

1/2 red bell pepper, thinly sliced

1/2 yellow bell pepper, thinly sliced

2 cups chicken broth, divided

1/4 teaspoon crushed red pepper flakes

DIRECTIONS

1. Bring a large pot of lightly salted water to a boil. Cook ravioli in boiling water for 8 to 10 minutes, or until done; drain.

2. Heat olive oil in large skillet over medium heat. Sauté onion and bell peppers until tender. Add one cup of the broth, season with pepper flakes, and simmer 5 minutes. Stir in remaining broth, and cook until most of broth has evaporated. Spoon pepper mixture over ravioli.

Alfredo Blue

Submitted by: **Melanie**

Makes: 8 servings

Preparation: 10 minutes

Cooking: 25 minutes

Ready In: 35 minutes

"This is the best alfredo sauce I have ever come up with and any kind of meat or vegetable can be added to it."

INGREDIENTS

1 (16 ounce) package fettuccine pasta

1 tablespoon olive oil

1 clove garlic, sliced

4 ounces blue cheese, crumbled

¼ cup grated Parmesan cheese

2 cups heavy cream

1 tablespoon Italian seasoning

salt and pepper to taste

DIRECTIONS

1. Bring a large pot of lightly salted water to a boil. Cook pasta in boiling water for 8 to 10 minutes, or until al dente; drain.

2. Heat olive oil in a small skillet over medium heat. Sauté garlic in olive oil until golden. Remove garlic, and reserve oil.

3. In a medium saucepan over medium-low heat, combine blue cheese, Parmesan cheese, and cream. Stir until cheeses are melted. Stir in the oil from the garlic pan. Season with Italian seasoning, salt, and pepper.

4. Toss sauce with hot pasta, and let stand 5 minutes before serving.

Angel Hair with Feta and Sun-Dried Tomatoes

Submitted by: **Nicole Faust Hunt**

Makes: 8 servings

Preparation: 15 minutes

Cooking: 15 minutes

Ready In: 30 minutes

"My husband begs me to make this dish. It is a surprisingly great mixture of flavors. You'll love it! Feel free to tailor the ingredient amounts to your taste. This is how we like it, but it is quite flexible."

INGREDIENTS

1 (16 ounce) package angel hair pasta

¼ cup olive oil

4 cloves garlic, crushed

3 ounces sun-dried tomatoes, softened and chopped

1 (8 ounce) package tomato basil feta cheese, crumbled

1 cup grated Parmesan cheese

1 bunch fresh cilantro, chopped

salt and pepper to taste

DIRECTIONS

1. Bring a large pot of lightly salted water to a boil. Cook pasta in boiling water until done; drain. Return pasta to the pot.

2. Mix in olive oil, garlic, tomatoes, feta, and Parmesan cheese. Stir in cilantro and season with salt and pepper. Serve warm.

Suki's Spinach and Feta Pasta

Submitted by: **Suki**

Makes: 4 servings

Preparation: 25 minutes

Cooking: 15 minutes

Ready In: 40 minutes

"Spinach, tomatoes, and mushrooms mingle with tangy feta cheese in this quick and easy dish for a summer night or anytime."

INGREDIENTS

1 (8 ounce) package penne pasta

2 tablespoons olive oil

½ cup chopped onion

1 clove garlic, minced

3 cups chopped tomatoes

1 cup sliced fresh mushrooms

2 cups spinach leaves, packed

salt and pepper to taste

1 pinch red pepper flakes

8 ounces feta cheese, crumbled

DIRECTIONS

1. Bring a large pot of lightly salted water to a boil. Cook pasta in boiling water until al dente; drain.

2. Meanwhile, heat olive oil in a large skillet over medium-high heat; add onion and garlic, and cook until golden brown. Mix in tomatoes, mushrooms, and spinach. Season with salt, pepper, and red pepper flakes. Cook 2 minutes more, until tomatoes are heated through and spinach is wilted. Reduce heat to medium, stir in pasta and feta cheese, and cook until heated through.

Spicy Pasta

Submitted by: **Donna Barry**

Makes: 6 servings

Preparation: 10 minutes

Cooking: 20 minutes

Ready In: 30 minutes

"This is a fiery but quick and easy to make pasta dish. For a milder flavor, simply leave out the chiles."

INGREDIENTS

1 (12 ounce) package rotini pasta

1 tablespoon vegetable oil

1 clove garlic, crushed

1 teaspoon dried basil

1 teaspoon Italian seasoning

1 onion, diced

2 red chile peppers, seeded and chopped

1 (14.5 ounce) can diced tomatoes

3 drops hot pepper sauce

salt and ground black pepper to taste

DIRECTIONS

1. Bring a large pot of lightly salted water to a boil. Cook pasta in boiling water for 8 to 10 minutes, or until al dente; drain.

2. Meanwhile, heat oil in a saucepan over medium heat. Sauté garlic with basil and Italian seasoning for 2 to 3 minutes. Stir in onion and chiles; cook until onion is tender. Stir in tomatoes and hot sauce; simmer for 5 minutes, or until heated through. Toss with the cooked pasta, and season with salt and pepper.

Chuck's Favorite Mac and Cheese

Submitted by: **Carla**

Makes: 6 servings

Preparation: 10 minutes

Cooking: 45 minutes

Ready In: 55 minutes

"Easily doubled for a potluck, cottage cheese and sour cream are the unique elements to this macaroni and cheese recipe."

INGREDIENTS

1 (8 ounce) package elbow macaroni

1 (8 ounce) package shredded sharp Cheddar cheese

1 (12 ounce) container small curd cottage cheese

1 (8 ounce) container sour cream

¼ cup grated Parmesan cheese

salt and pepper to taste

1 cup dry bread crumbs

¼ cup butter, melted

DIRECTIONS

1. Preheat oven to 350°F (175°C). Bring a large pot of lightly salted water to a boil, add pasta, and cook until done; drain.

2. In 9x13 inch baking dish, stir together macaroni, shredded Cheddar cheese, cottage cheese, sour cream, Parmesan cheese, salt and pepper. In a small bowl, mix together bread crumbs and melted butter. Sprinkle topping over macaroni mixture.

3. Bake 30 to 35 minutes, or until top is golden.

Orzo with Mushrooms and Walnuts

Submitted by: **Amanda**

Makes: 8 servings

Preparation: 10 minutes

Cooking: 25 minutes

Ready In: 35 minutes

"This recipe makes quite a bit. Everyone I've prepared it for loves it. You can easily cut the recipe in half."

INGREDIENTS

⅓ cup chopped walnuts

3 tablespoons olive oil

2 onions, chopped

1 pound fresh mushrooms, sliced

4 cups chicken broth

2 cups uncooked orzo pasta

salt and pepper to taste

DIRECTIONS

1. Preheat the oven to 350°F (175°C). Place walnuts on a baking sheet. Bake for 8 to 10 minutes in the preheated oven, or until they release their aroma. Stir once or twice for even toasting.

2. Heat oil in a large heavy saucepan over medium-high heat. Sauté onion and mushrooms until tender and golden brown.

3. Pour in broth, and bring to a boil. Stir in orzo, reduce heat to low, and cover. Simmer until orzo is tender and liquid is absorbed, about 15 minutes. If after 15 minutes there is still liquid, remove cover, and cook until liquid is gone. Remove from heat, and stir in walnuts. Season with salt and pepper to taste.

seafood

Can't find a recipe you like for the type of fish you want to cook? Good news: In these recipes, any variety of fish can easily be substituted for another kind with a similar texture. Use those frozen filets left over from last month's fishing trip, and remember to adjust the cooking time for thicker or thinner pieces of fish. Most of the shrimp you see at the fish counter has been previously frozen, so cut out the middleman and buy it frozen yourself; in the long run it's fresher, cheaper and more convenient.

Tequila Shrimp

Submitted by: **Michael**

Makes: 6 servings

Preparation: 10 minutes

Cooking: 10 minutes

Ready In: 20 minutes

"This is a very simple and excellent recipe. Goes great over pasta."

INGREDIENTS

2 tablespoons unsalted butter

4 cloves garlic, chopped

1½ pounds large shrimp - peeled and deveined

½ cup tequila

½ cup chopped fresh cilantro

salt and pepper to taste

DIRECTIONS

1. Melt butter in a large skillet over medium heat. Sauté garlic until light brown. Place shrimp in the pan, and cook for 3 minutes.

2. Pour in tequila, and season with cilantro, salt, and pepper. Cook for 2 more minutes.

Lemon Pepper Shrimp with Mustard

Submitted by: **Brenda Bolliver**

Makes: 8 servings

Preparation: 10 minutes

Cooking: 10 minutes

Ready In: 20 minutes

"Quick, easy dish to make during the week, or anytime. Even though it takes very little time to prepare, it's good enough for guests!"

INGREDIENTS

½ cup butter

3 cloves garlic, minced

¼ cup white wine

1 teaspoon lemon pepper

2 tablespoons prepared yellow mustard

¼ teaspoon red pepper flakes

2 pounds fresh shrimp, peeled and deveined

1 tablespoon chopped fresh parsley

DIRECTIONS

1. Melt butter in a large skillet over medium heat. Sauté garlic in butter until tender, 1 to 2 minutes. Pour in the wine. Season with lemon pepper, mustard, and red pepper flakes. Stir in shrimp, and cook 5 minutes, or until shrimp is done. Sprinkle with chopped parsley.

Clams Italiano

Submitted by: **Bonnie Dailey**

Makes: 6 servings

Preparation: 15 minutes

Cooking: 15 minutes

Ready In: 30 minutes

"These clams are steamed in wine, butter, and herbs. When the clams are gone, dip Italian bread in the broth."

INGREDIENTS

½ cup butter

5 cloves garlic, minced

2 cups dry white wine

1 tablespoon dried oregano

1 tablespoon dried parsley

1 teaspoon crushed red pepper flakes (optional)

36 small clams in shell, scrubbed

DIRECTIONS

1. Melt butter in a large skillet over medium heat. Cook garlic in butter briefly. Stir in wine, and season with oregano, parsley, and red pepper flakes.

2. Place clams in the wine mixture. Cover, and steam until all the clams have opened: discard any that do not open. Serve in soup bowls, and ladle broth generously over them.

Crabbies

Submitted by: **Tracy Clark**

Makes: 8 servings

Preparation: 10 minutes

Cooking: 10 minutes

Ready In: 20 minutes

"My mom gave me this recipe. It was a childhood favorite! Crabby, cheesy, tasty! You can freeze the mixture if you want, and then thaw and use as needed."

INGREDIENTS

¼ cup margarine, softened

⅔ (5 ounce) container sharp processed cheese spread

8 ounces cooked crabmeat

¼ cup mayonnaise

½ teaspoon garlic powder

½ teaspoon dried parsley

8 English muffins, split

DIRECTIONS

1. Preheat oven on broiler setting.

2. In a medium bowl, mix together margarine and cheese spread. Stir in crabmeat, mayonnaise, garlic powder, and parsley. Spread the mixture on the split English muffins. Arrange on a cookie sheet.

3. Broil until the cheese mixture is bubbly.

Maryland Crab Cakes III

Submitted by: **Jeff Hemerly**

"These crab cakes are rich and moist with lots of meat and very little filling. Typical of finer restaurants!"

INGREDIENTS

1⅛ cups crushed saltine crackers

1 cup mayonnaise

1 teaspoon prepared brown mustard

¼ cup chopped onion

1 stalk celery, chopped

1 teaspoon Old Bay® Seasoning

1 pound crabmeat

DIRECTIONS

1. Preheat oven on broiler setting. Lightly grease a baking sheet.

2. In a medium bowl, mix together crushed saltine crackers, mayonnaise, brown mustard, onion, celery, and Old Bay seasoning. Gently stir in the crabmeat. Shape into 6 patties. Place on prepared baking sheet.

3. Broil crab cakes 8 to 10 minutes on each side, or until golden brown.

Super Easy Salmon Cakes

Submitted by: **Marianna**

Makes: 4 servings

Preparation: 15 minutes

Cooking: 10 minutes

Ready In: 25 minutes

"This recipe is a great way to used canned or leftover salmon, and is easily adapted to include whatever spices you like."

INGREDIENTS

1 (7 ounce) can salmon, drained and flaked

1 egg, beaten

1 tablespoon olive oil

2 green onions, finely chopped

2 cups finely crushed saltine cracker crumbs

lemon pepper to taste

DIRECTIONS

1. Preheat oven to 375 °F (190°C).

2. In a medium bowl, mix together salmon, egg, olive oil, green onions, and ⅔ cup cracker crumbs. Season with lemon pepper. Form mixture into 8 patties. Coat patties with remaining cracker crumbs, and arrange in a single layer on a baking sheet.

3. Bake 10 minutes in the preheated oven, turning once, or until golden brown on both sides.

Pan Seared Salmon

Submitted by: **Pat**

Makes: 4 servings

Preparation: 10 minutes

Cooking: 10 minutes

Ready In: 20 minutes

"Simply seasoned with salt and pepper, these salmon fillets are pan seared with capers, and garnished with slices of lemon."

INGREDIENTS

4 (6 ounce) fillets salmon

2 tablespoons olive oil

2 tablespoons capers

$\frac{1}{8}$ teaspoon salt

$\frac{1}{8}$ teaspoon ground black pepper

4 slices lemon

DIRECTIONS

1. Preheat a large heavy skillet over medium heat for 3 minutes.

2. Coat salmon with olive oil. Place in skillet, and increase heat to high. Cook for 3 minutes. Sprinkle with capers, and salt and pepper. Turn salmon over, and cook for 5 minutes, or until browned. Salmon is done when it flakes easily with a fork.

3. Transfer salmon to individual plates, and garnish with lemon slices.

Salmon with Brown Sugar and Bourbon Glaze

Makes: 4 servings

Preparation: 5 minutes

Cooking: 15 minutes

Ready In: 20 minutes

Submitted by: **Debbie F**

"This is a simple and delicious way to serve salmon. It is very pretty and good served with brown rice and fresh asparagus."

INGREDIENTS

4 tablespoons butter

½ cup dark brown sugar

4 (6 ounce) salmon steaks

⅓ cup bourbon whiskey

DIRECTIONS

1. Melt butter in a large heavy skillet over medium heat. Stir in brown sugar. Place salmon fillets on top of brown sugar mixture. Cook for 5 minutes on medium heat. Turn salmon, and pour bourbon around the fillets. Continue cooking for 5 minutes, or until fish flakes easily with a fork. Spoon glaze over the salmon, and serve.

Salmon with Pecan Honey Glaze

Submitted by: **Kimber**

Makes: 4 servings

Preparation: 5 minutes

Cooking: 30 minutes

Ready In: 35 minutes

"Beautiful, crispy salmon fillets with a honey-pecan glaze that is easy and delicious!"

INGREDIENTS

1 cup pecan halves or pieces

1 cup honey

3/4 cup butter

1/4 cup vegetable oil

4 (6 ounce) fillets salmon

salt and pepper to taste

DIRECTIONS

1. Preheat oven to 350°F (175°C). Spread pecans in a single layer on a baking sheet. Bake 8 to 10 minutes, or until slightly browned. Stir 2 or 3 times to toast uniformly.

2. In a small saucepan over medium-high heat, combine honey with half of the butter. Stir in the toasted pecans, and cook for 8 to 10 minutes to infuse the flavors. Remove from heat, and keep warm.

3. Melt remaining butter with oil in a large skillet over high heat. Season fish with salt and pepper. Arrange fillets in skillet, and cook until firm to the touch, about 4 to 5 minutes per side. Salmon is done when it flakes easily with a fork. Transfer to serving plate, and spoon glaze over top.

Baked Salmon Fillets Dijon

Submitted by: **Christine Johnson**

Makes: 4 servings

Preparation: 10 minutes

Cooking: 15 minutes

Ready In: 25 minutes

"Delicious baked salmon coated with Dijon-style mustard and seasoned bread crumbs, and topped with butter."

INGREDIENTS

4 (4 ounce) fillets salmon

3 tablespoons prepared Dijon-style mustard

salt and pepper to taste

¼ cup Italian-style dry bread crumbs

¼ cup butter, melted

DIRECTIONS

1. Preheat oven to 400°F (200°C). Line a shallow baking pan with aluminum foil.

2. Place salmon skin-side down on foil. Spread a thin layer of mustard on the top of each fillet, and season with salt and pepper. Top with bread crumbs, then drizzle with melted butter.

3. Bake in a preheated oven for 15 minutes, or until salmon flakes easily with a fork.

Baked Dijon Salmon

Submitted by: **Arnie Williams**

Makes: 4 servings

Preparation: 20 minutes

Cooking: 15 minutes

Ready In: 35 minutes

"This is a wonderful way to prepare fresh salmon fillets in the oven. Be sure to make extra, your family will be begging for more!"

INGREDIENTS

¼ cup butter, melted

3 tablespoons Dijon mustard

1½ tablespoons honey

¼ cup dry bread crumbs

¼ cup finely chopped pecans

4 teaspoons chopped fresh parsley

4 (4 ounce) fillets salmon

salt and pepper to taste

1 lemon, for garnish

DIRECTIONS

1. Preheat oven to 400°F (200°C).

2. In a small bowl, stir together butter, mustard, and honey. Set aside. In another bowl, mix together bread crumbs, pecans, and parsley.

3. Brush each salmon fillet lightly with honey mustard mixture, and sprinkle the tops of the fillets with the bread crumb mixture.

4. Bake salmon 12 to 15 minutes in the preheated oven, or until it flakes easily with a fork. Season with salt and pepper, and garnish with a wedge of lemon.

Salmon with Dill

Submitted by: **John Bragg**

Makes: 4 servings

Preparation: 5 minutes

Cooking: 25 minutes

Ready In: 30 minutes

"This is a simple recipe for salmon fillets or salmon steaks. With just a hint of seasoning, you can bring out the delicious taste of the salmon. Serve with tartar sauce and lemon."

INGREDIENTS

1 pound salmon fillets or steaks

1/4 teaspoon salt

1/2 teaspoon ground black pepper

1 teaspoon onion powder

1 teaspoon dried dill weed

2 tablespoons butter

DIRECTIONS

1. Preheat oven to 400°F (200°C).

2. Rinse salmon, and arrange in a 9x13 inch baking dish. Sprinkle salt, pepper, onion powder, and dill over the fish. Place pieces of butter evenly over the fish.

3. Bake in preheated oven for 20 to 25 minutes. Salmon is done when it flakes easily with a fork.

Pan Seared Red Snapper

Submitted by: **Katie**

Makes: 2 servings

Preparation: 10 minutes

Cooking: 10 minutes

Ready In: 20 minutes

"This is great for a gourmet taste on a tight schedule. Also, my husband, who isn't a fish fan, requests this recipe! Drizzle sauce over fish, and serve with vegetables."

INGREDIENTS

2 (4 ounce) fillets red snapper

1 tablespoon olive oil

1 lemon, juiced

2 tablespoons rice wine vinegar

1 teaspoon Dijon mustard

1 tablespoon honey

1/4 cup chopped green onions

1 teaspoon ground ginger

DIRECTIONS

1. Rinse snapper under cold water, and pat dry. In a shallow bowl, mix together olive oil, lemon juice, rice vinegar, mustard, honey, green onions, and ginger.

2. Heat a non-stick skillet over medium heat. Dip snapper fillets in marinade to coat both sides, and place in skillet. Cook for 2 to 3 minutes on each side. Pour remaining marinade into skillet. Reduce heat, and simmer for 2 to 3 minutes, or until fish flakes easily with a fork.

Cajun Style Blackened Snapper

Submitted by: **Sandra**

Makes: 4 servings

Preparation: 15 minutes

Cooking: 10 minutes

Ready In: 25 minutes

"Fillets of red snapper are coated with a mixture of pepper and herbs, then cooked at high heat until the coating blackens. Spicy and delicious!"

INGREDIENTS

2 tablespoons paprika

2 teaspoons cayenne pepper

1½ teaspoons ground white pepper

1½ teaspoons ground black pepper

1 tablespoon salt

2 teaspoons onion powder

2 teaspoons garlic powder

1 teaspoon dried thyme

1 teaspoon dried oregano

4 (6 ounce) fillets red snapper

1½ cups butter, melted

DIRECTIONS

1. In a small bowl, mix together paprika, cayenne pepper, white pepper, black pepper, salt, onion powder, garlic powder, thyme, and oregano.

2. Heat a large cast iron skillet over high heat for 10 minutes, or until extremely hot.

3. Dip fish into melted butter, and sprinkle each fillet generously with the seasoning mixture. Place the fish fillets in the hot skillet. Pour 1 tablespoon of butter over each fillet. Cook until the coating on the underside of the fillet turns black, 3 to 5 minutes. Turn the fish over. Pour another tablespoon of butter over the fish, and cook for 2 minutes, or until fish flakes easily with a fork.

Light and Spicy Fish

Submitted by: **Matt Adams**

Makes: 2 servings

Preparation: 5 minutes

Cooking: 20 minutes

Ready In: 25 minutes

"This recipe is easy to make and very healthy. You may substitute other firm-fleshed fish such as ocean perch or grouper."

INGREDIENTS

2 (6 ounce) fillets red snapper

¼ teaspoon garlic powder

salt and ground black pepper to taste

¼ cup picante sauce

½ lime, juiced

DIRECTIONS

1. Preheat oven to 350°F (175°C). Place a sheet of aluminum foil onto a baking sheet, and grease lightly.

2. Place fillets onto the foil, and sprinkle with garlic powder, salt, and pepper. Spoon picante sauce over fillets, and squeeze lime juice over the top. Bring the sides of the foil together, and fold the seam to seal in the fish.

3. Bake in preheated oven for 15 to 20 minutes, or until fish flakes easily with a fork.

Red Snapper Livornese

Submitted by: **Ro**

Makes: 4 servings

Preparation: 20 minutes

Cooking: 25 minutes

Ready In: 45 minutes

"A tangy, easy recipe for almost any firm-fleshed fish fillets: red snapper, sea bass, grouper. Adaptable for sole, flounder, tilapia, and other thin fillets by adjusting cooking time. Serve with white rice or couscous, and a salad or steamed broccoli."

INGREDIENTS

2 tablespoons olive oil

1/2 small onion, diced

2 cloves garlic, minced

5 whole canned tomatoes, drained and chopped

2 tablespoons capers, chopped

1/2 cup sliced black olives, drained

1/4 teaspoon crushed red pepper flakes

1/2 tablespoon chopped fresh parsley

1 pound red snapper fillets

1 tablespoon fresh lemon juice

DIRECTIONS

1. Preheat oven to 400°F (200°C).

2. In a medium skillet, heat olive oil and sauté onion until tender, about 5 minutes. Add garlic, and sauté for 1 minute. Stir in tomatoes, capers, black olives, red pepper flakes, and parsley. Bring to a boil, and simmer for 10 minutes.

3. Spread ½ cup of the sauce in a 11x7 inch baking dish, and arrange the snapper fillets in a single layer in the dish. Drizzle lemon juice over the fillets, and then pour the remaining sauce over all.

4. Bake for 15 minutes for ½ inch thick fillets, or 30 minutes for 1 inch thick fillets. Baste once with the sauce while baking. Snapper is done when it flakes easily with a fork.

Blackened Tuna

Submitted by: **Denys**

Makes: 6 servings

Preparation: 10 minutes

Cooking: 10 minutes

Ready In: 20 minutes

"It may seem simple, but it's my favorite way to have tuna. Seared fish steaks are a Cajun tradition."

INGREDIENTS

1½ pounds fresh tuna steaks, 1 inch thick

2 tablespoons Cajun seasoning

2 tablespoons olive oil

2 tablespoons butter

DIRECTIONS

1. Generously coat tuna with Cajun seasoning.

2. Heat oil and butter in a large skillet over high heat. When oil is nearly smoking, place steaks in pan. Cook on one side for 3 to 4 minutes, or until blackened. Turn steaks, and cook for 3 to 4 minutes, or to desired doneness.

Steamed Tuna Fish

Submitted by: **Janice Laughton**

Makes: 8 servings

Preparation: 20 minutes

Cooking: 10 minutes

Ready In: 30 minutes

"Tender steamed tuna with a ginger, sherry, garlic and soy sauce."

INGREDIENTS

2 pounds fresh tuna steaks

1/2 cup soy sauce

1/2 cup sherry

1/2 cup vegetable oil

1 bunch green onions, finely chopped

1/2 cup minced fresh ginger root

3 cloves garlic, minced

1 teaspoon salt

1 teaspoon ground black pepper

DIRECTIONS

1. Place tuna steaks in a steamer over 1 inch of boiling water, and cover. Cook 6 to 8 minutes, or until fish flakes easily with a fork.

2. Meanwhile, in a medium saucepan, combine soy sauce, sherry, vegetable oil, green onions, ginger, garlic, salt, and black pepper. Bring to a boil.

3. Remove tuna steaks from steamer, and place in a serving dish. Pour sauce over tuna steaks, and serve immediately.

Grilled Tuna Teriyaki

Submitted by: **Maridele**

Makes: 4 servings

Preparation: 15 minutes

Cooking: 10 minutes

Ready In: 55 minutes

"Delicious right off the grill! Take care not to overcook the steaks, as tuna can quickly become quite dry."

INGREDIENTS

2 tablespoons light soy sauce

1 tablespoon Chinese rice wine

1 clove garlic, minced

1 tablespoon minced fresh ginger root

4 (6 ounce) tuna steaks (about ¾ inch thick)

1 tablespoon vegetable oil

DIRECTIONS

1. In a shallow dish, combine soy sauce, rice wine, garlic, and ginger. Place tuna in the marinade, and turn to coat. Cover, and refrigerate for at least 30 minutes.

2. Preheat grill for medium-high heat, and lightly oil grate.

3. Discard the marinade, and pat tuna steaks dry with paper towels. Brush both sides with oil.

4. Place tuna steaks on the grill. Cook for approximately 3 minutes on each side, or to your desired doneness.

Grilled Teriyaki Tuna

Submitted by: **Steve Dreibelbis**

Makes: 4 servings
Preparation: 5 minutes
Cooking: 10 minutes
Ready In: 45 minutes

"Yellowfin tuna is always delicious when grilled. This is great at a tail-gate party, or at your Saturday afternoon summer barbecue. You can add a little cayenne pepper or minced fresh ginger to the marinade to give it a little extra kick."

INGREDIENTS

1 cup teriyaki sauce

3/4 cup olive oil

2 tablespoons minced garlic

1 teaspoon ground black pepper

4 (4 ounce) fillets yellowfin tuna

DIRECTIONS

1. In a large resealable plastic bag, combine the teriyaki sauce, oil, garlic, and pepper. Place the tuna fillets in the bag. Seal the bag with as little air in it as possible. Give the mix a good shake, to ensure the tuna fillets are well coated. Marinate for 30 minutes in the refrigerator.

2. Meanwhile, preheat an outdoor grill for high heat, and lightly oil grate.

3. Remove tuna from marinade, and place on grill. For rare tuna, grill for 3 to 5 minutes on each side. For medium, grill 5 to 8 minutes per side. For well done, grill for 8 to 10 minutes per side.

Sea Bass Cuban Style

Submitted by: **Kiki Hahn**

Makes: 4 servings

Preparation: 20 minutes

Cooking: 25 minutes

Ready In: 45 minutes

"Easy to prepare - sure to please. Great dish for guests when you have little time (or desire) to slave all day in the kitchen."

INGREDIENTS

2 tablespoons extra virgin olive oil

1½ cups thinly sliced white onions

2 tablespoons minced garlic

4 cups seeded, chopped plum tomatoes

1½ cups dry white wine

⅔ cup sliced stuffed green olives

¼ cup drained capers

⅛ teaspoon red pepper flakes

4 (6 ounce) fillets sea bass

2 tablespoons butter

¼ cup chopped fresh cilantro

DIRECTIONS

1. Heat oil in a large skillet over medium heat. Sauté onions until soft. Stir in garlic, and sauté about 1 minute. Add tomatoes, and cook until they begin to soften. Stir in wine, olives, capers, and red pepper flakes. Heat to a simmer.

2. Place sea bass into sauce. Cover, and gently simmer for 10 to 12 minutes, or until fish flakes easily with a fork. Transfer fish to a serving plate, and keep warm.

3. Increase the heat, and add butter to sauce. Simmer until the sauce thickens. Stir in cilantro. Serve sauce over fish.

Sea Bass with Honeyed Apples

Submitted by: **Lola**

Makes: 4 servings

Preparation: 20 minutes

Cooking: 15 minutes

Ready In: 35 minutes

"Crispy fried fish topped with honeyed apples. This unique dish always get loads of compliments. Plus everyone is always surprised of the pairing of fish and apples. If you can't get sea bass, any firm white-fleshed fish will work. Catfish is another fish that goes great with the apples."

INGREDIENTS

4 apples - peeled, cored and cut into thin wedges

1/2 cup margarine, divided

1/4 cup honey

1/4 cup all-purpose flour

1/4 teaspoon salt

1/4 teaspoon ground black pepper

2 cups dried bread crumbs

1 egg, beaten

4 (6 ounce) fillets sea bass

DIRECTIONS

1. Melt 1/4 cup of the margarine in a large skillet over medium-high heat. Fry the apples in margarine until tender. Stir in honey, reduce heat, and keep warm.

2. In a shallow bowl, mix together flour, salt, and pepper. Place bread crumbs in another shallow bowl, and egg in a third bowl.

3. Melt the remaining 1/4 cup margarine in a large skillet over medium heat. Dredge the fish in the seasoned flour, dip in egg, then coat with bread crumbs. Place the coated fillets in the hot skillet, and cook for about 3 to 4 minutes per side. The fillets should be nicely browned, and they should flake easily with a fork. Place fish on a serving dish, and spoon the apples with honey over the top of each fillet.

Lemon-Orange Orange Roughy

Submitted by: **Brian Ehrler**

Makes: 4 servings

Preparation: 15 minutes

Cooking: 5 minutes

Ready In: 20 minutes

"Orange roughy fillets with a citrus twist. Very quick to prepare."

INGREDIENTS

1 tablespoon olive oil

4 (4 ounce) fillets orange roughy

1 orange, juiced

1 lemon, juiced

½ teaspoon lemon pepper

DIRECTIONS

1. Heat oil in a large skillet over medium-high heat. Arrange fillets in the skillet, and drizzle with orange juice and lemon juice. Sprinkle with lemon pepper. Cook for 5 minutes, or until fish is easily flaked with a fork.

allrecipes tried & true quick and easy | seafood

Baked Orange Roughy Italian-Style

Submitted by: **Tonya Dennis**

Makes: 4 servings

Preparation: 15 minutes

Cooking: 15 minutes

Ready In: 30 minutes

"The flavor of this delicate fish is enhanced with Italian-style seasonings that are sure to please even the pickiest eater. Quick, easy, and simply delicious."

INGREDIENTS

1/4 cup Italian seasoned bread crumbs

2 tablespoons grated Parmesan cheese

2 tablespoons grated Romano cheese

1/4 teaspoon garlic powder

1/2 teaspoon salt, or to taste

1 pound orange roughy fillets

1/4 cup butter, melted

1 tablespoon chopped fresh parsley

DIRECTIONS

1. Preheat oven to 400°F (200°C). Coat a medium baking dish with non-stick cooking spray.

2. In a shallow bowl, mix bread crumbs, Parmesan cheese, Romano cheese, garlic powder, and salt.

3. Brush both sides of orange roughy fillets with butter, and dredge in the bread crumb mixture. Arrange fillets in a single layer in the prepared baking dish, and sprinkle with parsley.

4. Bake in preheated oven 10 to 15 minutes, or until the fish flakes easily with a fork.

Dijon Crusted Halibut

Submitted by: **Christine Johnson**

Makes: 4 servings

Preparation: 15 minutes

Cooking: 15 minutes

Ready In: 30 minutes

"Delightful baked halibut breaded with a spicy mixture of Dijon mustard, horseradish, fresh Parmesan cheese and bread crumbs."

INGREDIENTS

¼ cup mayonnaise

1 tablespoon prepared Dijon-style mustard

1 tablespoon prepared horseradish

1 tablespoon fresh lemon juice

¼ cup dry bread crumbs

1 tablespoon grated Parmesan cheese

4 (4 ounce) fillets halibut

1 tablespoon margarine, melted

¼ cup dry bread crumbs

1 tablespoon grated Parmesan cheese

DIRECTIONS

1. Preheat oven to 350°F (175°C). Lightly grease a baking sheet.

2. In a small bowl, mix together mayonnaise, mustard, horseradish, and lemon juice. Stir in ¼ cup bread crumbs and 1 tablespoon Parmesan cheese. Arrange fish fillets on the prepared baking sheet. Spread bread crumb mixture evenly over fish.

3. In a small bowl, mix together melted margarine, ¼ cup bread crumbs, and 1 tablespoon Parmesan cheese. Sprinkle over the coated halibut.

4. Bake for 15 to 18 minutes, or until fish flakes easily with a fork.

Barbeque Halibut Steaks

Submitted by: **Duane Glende**

Makes: 2 servings

Preparation: 15 minutes

Cooking: 15 minutes

Ready In: 30 minutes

"A simple recipe for barbecued halibut. Soy sauce and brown sugar add a special zip that is uncommonly delicious."

INGREDIENTS

2 tablespoons butter

2 tablespoons brown sugar

2 cloves garlic, minced

1 tablespoon lemon juice

2 teaspoons soy sauce

½ teaspoon ground black pepper

1 (1 pound) halibut steak

DIRECTIONS

1. Preheat an outdoor grill for medium-high heat, and lightly oil grate.

2. Combine butter, brown sugar, garlic, lemon juice, soy sauce, and pepper in a small saucepan. Cook over medium heat until the sugar dissolves.

3. Coat the halibut with sauce, and place on the grill. Grill for 5 minutes on each side, basting frequently, or until fish flakes easily with a fork.

Beer Batter Fish Made Great

Submitted by: **Linda Olar**

Makes: 8 servings

Preparation: 15 minutes

Cooking: 15 minutes

Ready In: 30 minutes

"This is a great beer batter fish recipe, and is very easy to do. We often fish all day with friends, and then cook the fish afterwards out on deck. Yummy and great!"

INGREDIENTS

2 quarts vegetable oil for frying

8 (4 ounce) fillets cod

salt and pepper to taste

1 cup all-purpose flour

2 tablespoons garlic powder

2 tablespoons paprika

2 teaspoons salt

2 teaspoons ground black pepper

1 egg, beaten

1 (12 fluid ounce) can or bottle beer

DIRECTIONS

1. Heat oil in a deep fryer to 365°F (185°C). Rinse fish, pat dry, and season with salt and pepper.

2. Combine flour, garlic powder, paprika, 2 teaspoons salt, and 2 teaspoons pepper. Stir egg into dry ingredients. Gradually mix in beer until a thin batter is formed. You should be able to see the fish through the batter after it has been dipped.

3. Dip fish fillets into the batter, then drop one at a time into hot oil. Fry fish, turning once, until both sides are golden brown. Drain on paper towels, and serve warm.

Crispy Fish Fillets

Submitted by: **Kimber**

Makes: 4 servings

Preparation: 10 minutes

Cooking: 10 minutes

Ready In: 20 minutes

"Even people who aren't sure if they love fish will love these crunchy fillets! Quick and easy!"

INGREDIENTS

1 egg

2 tablespoons prepared yellow mustard

1/2 teaspoon salt

1 1/2 cups instant mashed potato flakes

1/4 cup oil for frying

4 (6 ounce) fillets sole

DIRECTIONS

1. In a shallow dish, whisk together the egg, mustard, and salt; set aside. Place the potato flakes in another shallow dish.

2. Heat oil in a large heavy skillet over medium-high heat.

3. Dip fish fillets in the egg mixture. Dredge the fillets in the potato flakes, making sure to completely coat the fish. For extra crispy, dip into egg and potato flakes again.

4. Fry fish fillets in oil for 3 to 4 minutes on each side, or until golden brown.

Fish in Foil

Submitted by: **Denyse**

Makes: 2 servings
Preparation: 10 minutes
Cooking: 20 minutes
Ready In: 30 minutes

"The 'no smell' fish recipe that is the ONLY one I make for my family (I hate fish, they LOVE it!). Take foil packets to table for service, and keep them around for the discarding of bones and skin. Then when dinner's done, haul those babies to the outside trash."

INGREDIENTS

2 rainbow trout fillets

1 tablespoon olive oil

2 teaspoons garlic salt

1 teaspoon ground black pepper

1 fresh jalapeno pepper, sliced

1 lemon, sliced

DIRECTIONS

1. Preheat oven to 400°F (200°C). Rinse fish, and pat dry.

2. Rub fillets with olive oil, and season with garlic salt and black pepper. Place each fillet on a large sheet of aluminum foil. Top with jalapeno slices, and squeeze the juice from the ends of the lemons over the fish. Arrange lemon slices on top of fillets. Carefully seal all edges of the foil to form enclosed packets. Place packets on baking sheet.

3. Bake in preheated oven for 15 to 20 minutes, depending on the size of fish. Fish is done when it flakes easily with a fork.

chicken and turkey

Want your poultry to be ready even faster? Buy boneless breasts or thighs, and either pound them thin with a mallet or cut them into bite-size slices before cooking. Leftover chicken and turkey have a million different uses, so next time you're preparing this versatile meat, throw in extra; you'll get a head start on one of the crowd-pleasing casserole, enchilada, pizza, salad, pasta, soup or sandwich recipes that follow. And remember, the biggest secret to tender, juicy chicken is *not* to overcook it!

Lemon Mushroom Herb Chicken

Submitted by: **Valerie Serao**

Makes: 4 servings

Preparation: 15 minutes

Cooking: 30 minutes

Ready In: 45 minutes

"Easy chicken and herbs in a creamy lemon and mushroom sauce. The sauce is excellent over rice – my kids can't get enough!"

INGREDIENTS

1 cup all-purpose flour

1/2 tablespoon dried thyme

2 tablespoons dried basil

1 tablespoon dried parsley

1 teaspoon paprika

1 teaspoon salt

1/2 teaspoon ground black pepper

1 teaspoon garlic powder

4 boneless, skinless chicken breast halves

1/2 cup butter

1 (10.75 ounce) can condensed cream of mushroom soup

1 (10.5 ounce) can condensed chicken broth

1/4 cup dry white wine

1 lemon, juiced

1 tablespoon chopped fresh parsley

2 tablespoons capers

1 tablespoon grated lemon zest

DIRECTIONS

1. In a shallow dish or bowl, combine the flour, thyme, basil, parsley, paprika, salt, ground black pepper, and garlic powder. Dredge chicken in the mixture to coat, patting off any excess flour.

2. Melt butter in a large skillet over medium heat, and cook chicken until no longer translucent. In a medium bowl, mix together the cream of mushroom soup, chicken broth, wine, and lemon juice; pour over chicken.

3. Cover skillet, and simmer 20 minutes, or until chicken is no longer pink and juices run clear. Garnish with parsley, capers, and lemon zest.

allrecipes tried & true quick and easy | chicken and turkey

Chicken Piccata III

Submitted by: **Sharon**

Makes: 4 servings

Preparation: 15 minutes

Cooking: 15 minutes

Ready In: 30 minutes

"This variation on the original uses mushrooms and artichoke hearts as a tasty twist. Yum! Serve over pasta or rice. White wine or water may be substituted for chicken broth."

INGREDIENTS

1 cup all-purpose flour

1/2 teaspoon paprika

salt and pepper to taste

1 pound boneless, skinless chicken breast halves, sliced into thin strips

1/4 cup vegetable oil

4 ounces fresh mushrooms, sliced

1/4 cup lemon juice

3/4 cup chicken stock

1/2 teaspoon garlic powder

1 (14 ounce) can artichoke hearts, drained and quartered

DIRECTIONS

1. In a shallow bowl, mix together flour, paprika, and salt and pepper. Dredge chicken pieces in the seasoned flour.

2. Heat oil in a large skillet over medium heat, and sauté chicken until light golden brown (about 45 seconds each side). Remove chicken from skillet, and set aside.

3. To skillet, add mushrooms, lemon juice, and chicken stock. Simmer until a smooth, light sauce develops. Season with garlic powder. Return chicken to the skillet, and simmer until chicken is no longer pink and juices run clear. Stir in artichoke hearts, and remove from heat.

Easier Chicken Marsala

Submitted by: **D. Alexander**

Makes: 4 servings

Preparation: 10 minutes

Cooking: 20 minutes

Ready In: 30 minutes

"Here's a lighter version of one of my favorite chicken dishes. For my family, this one's a keeper!"

INGREDIENTS

¼ cup all-purpose flour

½ teaspoon garlic salt

¼ teaspoon ground black pepper

½ teaspoon dried oregano

4 boneless, skinless chicken breast halves

1 tablespoon olive oil

1 tablespoon butter

1 cup sliced fresh mushrooms

½ cup Marsala wine

DIRECTIONS

1. In a medium bowl, stir together the flour, garlic salt, pepper, and oregano. Dredge chicken in the mixture to lightly coat.

2. Heat olive oil and butter in a large skillet over medium heat. Fry the chicken in the skillet for 2 minutes, or until lightly browned on one side. Turn chicken over, and add mushrooms. Cook about 2 minutes, until other side of chicken is lightly browned. Stir mushrooms so that they cook evenly.

3. Pour Marsala wine over the chicken. Cover skillet, and reduce heat to low; simmer for 10 minutes, or until chicken is no longer pink and juices run clear.

Chicken and Red Wine Sauce

Submitted by: **Robin**

Makes: 6 servings

Preparation: 10 minutes

Cooking: 45 minutes

Ready In: 55 minutes

"A simple red wine sauce with brown sugar, garlic, paprika, salt, and pepper makes this dish simply yummy! Braised chicken breasts, brazenly good taste."

INGREDIENTS

1 tablespoon olive oil

1 tablespoon minced garlic

3 pounds skinless, boneless chicken breast halves

1 tablespoon paprika

1 cup brown sugar

1 cup red wine

salt and pepper to taste

DIRECTIONS

1. Heat oil in a large skillet over medium high heat. Cook garlic in oil until tender. Place chicken in the skillet, and cook about 10 minutes on each side, until no longer pink and juices run clear.

2. Drain oil from skillet. Sprinkle chicken with paprika and 1 cup brown sugar. Pour red wine around chicken. Cover, and simmer about 15 to 20 minutes; lightly baste chicken with wine sauce while cooking. Season to taste with salt and pepper.

Chicken Pepper Steak

Submitted by: **Tiara**

Makes: 4 servings

Preparation: 15 minutes

Cooking: 30 minutes

Ready In: 45 minutes

"Chicken breast simmered with onion, bell pepper, tomatoes, soy sauce, and spices to be served with a rich, pepper steak-style gravy. If you like the taste of pepper steak but really don't enjoy red meat, try it with chicken!"

INGREDIENTS

1 tablespoon vegetable oil

1 pound skinless, boneless chicken breasts

1 teaspoon seasoning salt

1/2 teaspoon onion powder

2 teaspoons minced garlic

1/2 cup soy sauce, divided

1 large onion, cut into long slices

2 tablespoons cornstarch

2 1/2 cups water

1 green bell pepper, sliced

4 roma (plum) tomatoes, seeded and chopped

DIRECTIONS

1. Heat oil in a large skillet over medium heat. Season chicken with salt and onion powder, and place in skillet. Cook for about 5 to 7 minutes, then add the garlic, 4 tablespoons soy sauce, and half of the sliced onion. Cook until chicken is no longer pink, and the juices run clear.

2. Dissolve cornstarch in water in a small bowl, and blend into the chicken mixture. Stir in 4 tablespoons soy sauce, bell pepper, tomatoes, and remaining onion. Simmer until gravy has reached desired consistency.

Chicken Adobo II

Submitted by: **sherry52**

Makes: 6 servings

Preparation: 15 minutes

Cooking: 30 minutes

Ready In: 45 minutes

"This recipe is from the Philippines. My stepfather was a Filipino, and I learned a few recipes from his family."

INGREDIENTS

1 (2 to 3 pound) whole chicken, cut into pieces

¼ cup apple cider vinegar

¼ cup soy sauce

ground black pepper to taste

2 tablespoons olive oil

1 clove garlic, crushed

2 bay leaves

DIRECTIONS

1. Place chicken pieces in a large bowl. Pour vinegar and soy sauce over chicken, and season with ground black pepper to taste. Toss to coat.

2. Heat oil in a large skillet over medium heat, and brown garlic. Be careful not to burn garlic, as this will make the dish taste bitter. After browning garlic, remove it from the oil.

3. Place marinated chicken pieces in hot oil. Pour remaining marinade over all, and add bay leaves. Reduce heat to low, and cook chicken pieces for about 10 minutes on each side, or until no longer pink and juices run clear. The marinade will reduce, and make a nice gravy. Remove bay leaves, and serve immediately.

Sweet and Sour Chicken II

Submitted by: **Sal**

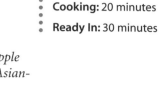

Makes: 6 servings

Preparation: 10 minutes

Cooking: 20 minutes

Ready In: 30 minutes

"A one pan dish of chicken, bell pepper, water chestnuts, and pineapple with a soy sauce, vinegar, and brown sugar sauce. Serve this tasty, Asian-inspired dish over hot rice!"

INGREDIENTS

1 (20 ounce) can pineapple chunks, juice reserved

¼ cup soy sauce

½ cup vinegar

¾ cup brown sugar

¼ cup all-purpose flour

1½ green bell peppers, diced

1 cup chopped celery

1 (8 ounce) can water chestnuts, drained and sliced

1½ pounds cooked chicken meat, cut into strips

DIRECTIONS

1. In a large saucepan over medium-low heat, blend reserved pineapple juice, soy sauce, vinegar, and brown sugar. Mix in flour, and stir until thickened.

2. Stir bell peppers, celery, and water chestnuts into the saucepan. Mix in chicken. Cook and stir until heated through. Stir in the pineapple chunks before serving.

Chicken Papadoris

Submitted by: **William Anatooskin**

Makes: 8 servings

Preparation: 20 minutes

Cooking: 30 minutes

Ready In: 50 minutes

"A delightful chicken recipe with a touch of curry. Serve Chicken Papadoris over cooked rice."

INGREDIENTS

¼ cup pine nuts

¼ cup butter

2 pounds skinless, boneless chicken breast halves, cut into bite size pieces

1 onion, chopped

4 cloves garlic, minced

2 tablespoons soy sauce

1 (14 ounce) can unsweetened coconut milk

1½ teaspoons paprika

¼ teaspoon ground cumin

1 teaspoon curry powder

2 teaspoons cornstarch

¼ cup cold water

DIRECTIONS

1. Heat a skillet over medium-high heat. Add pine nuts, and cook stirring frequently, until evenly toasted. Remove from heat, and set aside.

2. Melt butter in a large skillet over medium heat. Stir in the chicken, and cook 5 to 10 minutes, until no longer pink and juices run clear.

3. Stir onion and garlic into the skillet, and cook until tender. Stir in the pine nuts, soy sauce, and coconut milk. Season with paprika, cumin, and curry powder.

4. In a small bowl, blend the cornstarch and water. Mix into the skillet. Stir constantly until a thick gravy has formed.

Chicken Supreme IV

Submitted by: **Christie**

Makes: 4 servings

Preparation: 15 minutes

Cooking: 40 minutes

Ready In: 55 minutes

"Breaded chicken breasts are sautéed until golden, then baked with Jack cheese, mushrooms, and a white wine sauce. This delicious chicken dish was taught to me by my mother. It calls for white Zinfandel wine, and has an amazing flavor. It is guaranteed to be one of your favorites, too. This dish goes well with asparagus, and some kind of pasta side (we like to make angel hair pasta with garlic herb butter). Enjoy!!"

INGREDIENTS

1½ cups grated Parmesan cheese

3 eggs, beaten

1½ cups Italian-style seasoned bread crumbs

3 tablespoons vegetable oil

4 skinless, boneless chicken breast halves

2 cups white Zinfandel wine

2 cups sliced fresh mushrooms

3 cups shredded Monterey Jack cheese

DIRECTIONS

1. Preheat oven to 375°F (190°C). Lightly grease a medium baking dish.

2. Place Parmesan cheese, eggs, and bread crumbs in three separate small bowls. Heat the oil in a large skillet over medium-high heat. Dip each piece of chicken into the Parmesan cheese, then into the egg, then into the bread crumbs. Brown the chicken on both sides in the hot skillet, and then transfer them to the prepared baking dish.

3. Pour wine into skillet, and scrape up the browned bits. Add mushrooms and cook for 5 minutes, or until tender. Top each chicken breast with even amounts of Monterey Jack cheese, then spoon mushrooms over the cheese. Pour the remaining wine from the skillet over all. Cover dish with aluminum foil.

4. Bake 30 to 35 minutes in the preheated oven, or until chicken is no longer pink and juices run clear.

Chicken with Couscous

Submitted by: **Julianne Ture**

Makes: 4 servings

Preparation: 20 minutes

Cooking: 25 minutes

Ready In: 45 minutes

"A Mediterranean-flavored chicken and vegetable stew served over couscous. It's my all-time favorite, and it's delicious!"

INGREDIENTS

3¼ cups low-sodium chicken broth

1 cup quick-cooking couscous

2 tablespoons olive oil

4 boneless, skinless chicken breast halves, cubed

1 pinch ground black pepper

½ cup finely chopped jalapeno chile peppers

1 carrot, thinly sliced

1 zucchini, diced

3 green onions, thinly sliced

1½ teaspoons grated fresh ginger root

1½ teaspoons curry powder

½ teaspoon ground coriander seed

1 teaspoon cornstarch

DIRECTIONS

1. In a medium saucepan, bring 2 cups of the chicken broth to a boil. Stir in couscous and 1½ teaspoons of the olive oil. Turn off heat, cover, and let stand 10 minutes.

2. Heat 1 tablespoon olive oil in a medium skillet over medium heat. Stir in the chicken, season with pepper, and cook until no longer pink and juices run clear. Remove chicken from the skillet, and set aside.

3. Heat the remaining olive oil in the skillet over medium heat. Stir in the jalapeno peppers and carrot, and sauté about 2 minutes. Mix in the zucchini, green onions, ginger, and ¼ cup chicken broth. Continue to cook and stir until tender, about 5 minutes.

4. In a small bowl, blend the remaining 1 cup chicken broth with curry powder, coriander, and cornstarch. Pour over the vegetables. Return chicken to the skillet. Continue cooking about 2 minutes until chicken is coated and the broth mixture begins to thicken. Serve over the couscous.

Feta Chicken

Submitted by: **Debbie**

Makes: 6 servings

Preparation: 15 minutes

Cooking: 30 minutes

Ready In: 45 minutes

"Chicken wrapped around tomato-basil feta cheese - simple, succulent, and sensational."

INGREDIENTS

6 skinless, boneless chicken breast halves

6 ounces tomato basil feta cheese, crumbled

¼ cup Italian-style dry bread crumbs, divided

DIRECTIONS

1. Preheat oven to 350°F (175°C). Lightly grease a 9x13 inch baking dish.

2. Place chicken breasts between 2 pieces of waxed paper. Gently pound chicken with flat side of meat mallet or rolling pin until about ¼ inch thick; remove wax paper. Place 1 ounce of feta cheese in the center of each chicken breast, and fold in half.

3. Spread 2 tablespoons bread crumbs in the bottom of the prepared baking dish. Arrange chicken in the dish, and top with remaining bread crumbs.

4. Bake 25 to 30 minutes in the preheated oven, or until chicken is no longer pink and juices run clear.

Dijonnaise Chicken

Submitted by: **Teri**

Makes: 4 servings

Preparation: 15 minutes

Cooking: 30 minutes

Ready In: 45 minutes

"This is a baked chicken breast with a great mustard taste that you can bake alone or in a casserole dish with prepared wild rice."

INGREDIENTS

4 skinless, boneless chicken breast halves

¼ cup prepared Dijon mustard mayonnaise blend

¼ cup olive oil

1 tablespoon fresh lemon juice

1 teaspoon lemon pepper

1 teaspoon salt

1 teaspoon chicken bouillon

DIRECTIONS

1. Preheat oven to 350°F (175°C).

2. Place chicken in a 9x13 inch baking dish. In a medium bowl, mix the mustard-mayonnaise blend, olive oil, lemon juice, lemon pepper, salt, and bouillon. Pour the mixture over the chicken.

3. Bake 30 minutes in the preheated oven, or until chicken is no longer pink and juices run clear.

Texas Ranch Chicken

Submitted by: **Jan Kinnard**

Makes: 6 servings

Preparation: 10 minutes

Cooking: 35 minutes

Ready In: 45 minutes

"This is a baked chicken recipe I created as a single mother one night when the cupboard seemed bare. The kids love it, and have created their own variations. Variation: In place of dressing and mozzarella cheese, use sour cream and Cheddar cheese - slices or shredded."

INGREDIENTS

2 teaspoons olive oil

1½ pounds skinless, boneless chicken parts

1½ cups Ranch-style salad dressing

2 cups shredded mozzarella cheese

DIRECTIONS

1. Preheat oven to 350°F (175°C). Spread the olive oil in a 9x13 inch baking dish.

2. Arrange chicken in the dish, and cover with the dressing. It's best to place chicken pieces close together so that the cheese and the dressing do not burn on the bottom of the pan.

3. Bake for 20 minutes in the preheated oven. Remove from heat, top with mozzarella cheese, and return to the oven. Continue cooking for about 15 minutes, until the cheese is melted and lightly browned and the chicken is no longer pink and juices run clear.

Tender Onion Baked Chicken

Submitted by: **Kim**

Makes: 4 servings

Preparation: 5 minutes

Cooking: 40 minutes

Ready In: 45 minutes

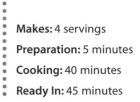

"Tender, tasty chicken breasts baked with butter, salt, pepper, and oniony seasoning. All ages like these - my 3 year old loves them! This can be served with mashed potatoes or with rice. Very tasty for the whole family."

INGREDIENTS

10 chicken breast tenderloins or strips

¼ cup margarine, melted

salt and pepper to taste

1 (1.5 ounce) envelope dry onion soup mix

DIRECTIONS

1. Preheat oven to 350°F (175°C).

2. Place chicken in a 9x13 inch baking dish. Pour melted margarine over the chicken strips. Season with salt and pepper, and sprinkle with dry onion soup mix.

3. Bake 40 minutes in the preheated oven, or until chicken is no longer pink and juices run clear.

Chicken Jerusalem II

Submitted by: **Kim**

Makes: 4 servings

Preparation: 5 minutes

Cooking: 40 minutes

Ready In: 45 minutes

"Chicken breasts with mushrooms and artichokes in a white wine cream sauce. This is my personal favorite. Serve with saffron rice, a green veggie of your choice, and the rest of the wine, of course! Enjoy!"

INGREDIENTS

4 skinless, boneless chicken breast halves

2 cups chicken stock

2 cloves garlic, crushed

1/2 small onion, finely chopped

1 cup white wine

1 (8 ounce) package sliced fresh mushrooms

1 (10 ounce) can artichoke hearts, drained

1 cup heavy cream

salt and pepper to taste

DIRECTIONS

1. Preheat oven to 325°F (165°C).

2. Place chicken in a 9x13 inch baking dish. Bake for 25 to 30 minutes, or until chicken is no longer pink and juices run clear.

3. While the chicken is baking, place the chicken stock, garlic, and onion in a medium saucepan. Bring to a boil, and cook until liquid is reduced by half. Stir in wine, and continue to cook until reduced and slightly thickened.

4. Add the mushrooms and artichokes to the chicken stock mixture. Reduce heat, and simmer until mushrooms are tender. Stir in the heavy cream, and cook, stirring occasionally, until thickened. Season with salt and pepper, and serve over the baked chicken.

allrecipes tried & true quick and easy | chicken and turkey

Weeknight Chicken Cordon Bleu

Submitted by: **Elaina**

Makes: 6 servings

Preparation: 15 minutes

Cooking: 25 minutes

Ready In: 40 minutes

"This is a tasty and quick recipe that is great for a weeknight when you want something yummy and don't have the time. Great over noodles."

INGREDIENTS

1 cup milk

1 cup dry bread crumbs

6 skinless, boneless chicken breast halves, pounded to ¼ inch thick

salt and pepper to taste

6 slices cooked ham

6 slices Swiss cheese

2 tablespoons vegetable oil

1 (10.5 ounce) can condensed cream of chicken soup

½ cup heavy cream

DIRECTIONS

1. Preheat oven to 350°F (175°C).

2. Place milk and bread crumbs in two separate shallow bowls. Season the chicken with salt and pepper. Place one slice of ham and one slice of cheese on each piece of chicken; roll, and secure with toothpicks. Dip each chicken roll into milk, and then into breadcrumbs.

3. Heat oil in a large skillet over medium-high heat. Brown rolled chicken on all sides. Arrange the chicken in a 9x13 inch baking dish.

4. In a small saucepan over medium heat, blend soup and cream; season with salt and pepper to taste. Pour over the chicken.

5. Bake in the preheated oven for 15 minutes, or until chicken is no longer pink and juices run clear.

Garlic Parmesan Chicken

Submitted by: **Jennifer**

Makes: 8 servings

Preparation: 15 minutes

Cooking: 40 minutes

Ready In: 55 minutes

"Awesome baked Chicken Parmesan! Chicken is dipped in garlic butter, then rolled in a cheese and bread crumb mixture, and baked to perfection."

INGREDIENTS

2 cups dry bread crumbs

1/2 cup grated Parmesan cheese

1 (3 ounce) can French-fried onions

1 teaspoon mustard powder

1/2 cup butter

2 cloves garlic, chopped

1 tablespoon Worcestershire sauce

8 chicken breast halves

DIRECTIONS

1. Preheat oven to 350°F (175°C). Lightly grease a 9x13 inch baking dish.

2. In a shallow dish or bowl, combine the bread crumbs, cheese, onions, and mustard powder; set aside. Melt butter in a small saucepan; add garlic and Worcestershire sauce, and sauté garlic until tender. Remove from heat.

3. Dip chicken breasts in garlic butter mixture, then roll in bread crumb and cheese mixture, coating thoroughly. Place coated chicken in the prepared baking dish. Drizzle with any remaining garlic butter mixture.

4. Bake in the preheated oven for 30 to 40 minutes, or until chicken is no longer pink and juices run clear.

Famous Butter Chicken

Submitted by: **Heather**

Makes: 4 servings

Preparation: 15 minutes

Cooking: 40 minutes

Ready In: 55 minutes

"Chicken breasts are dipped in beaten eggs and cracker crumbs, then baked with butter. These chicken breast are really tender and moist. Excellent flavor! I never have leftovers."

INGREDIENTS

2 eggs, beaten

1 cup crushed buttery round cracker crumbs

½ teaspoon garlic salt

ground black pepper to taste

4 skinless, boneless chicken breast halves

½ cup butter, cut into pieces

DIRECTIONS

1. Preheat oven to 375 °F (190°C).

2. Place eggs and cracker crumbs in two separate shallow bowls. Mix cracker crumbs with garlic salt and pepper. Dip chicken in the eggs, then dredge in the crumb mixture to coat.

3. Arrange coated chicken in a 9x13 inch baking dish. Place pieces of butter around the chicken.

4. Bake in the preheated oven for 40 minutes, or until chicken is no longer pink and juices run clear.

Four Seasons Enchiladas

Submitted by: **Janice Elder**

Makes: 8 servings

Preparation: 15 minutes

Cooking: 20 minutes

Ready In: 35 minutes

"Nice and spicy use for leftover turkey in a form that even the children will enjoy. Quick, too! Great topped with black olives, green onions, and tomatoes! Leftover ham would also be excellent in this dish."

INGREDIENTS

1 (4 ounce) can chopped green chile peppers, drained

4 ounces cream cheese, softened

1/2 teaspoon ground cumin

2 cups chopped cooked turkey

8 (8 inch) flour tortillas

1 (16 ounce) jar salsa

1 (16 ounce) can chili beans, undrained

1 cup shredded Monterey Jack cheese

DIRECTIONS

1. Preheat oven to 350°F (175°C). Lightly grease a 9x13 inch baking dish.

2. In a medium bowl, mix chile peppers, cream cheese, and cumin. Stir in chopped turkey.

3. Place the tortillas in a microwave oven. Heat for 1 minute, or until the tortillas are softened. Spread about 2 heaping tablespoons of the chile pepper mixture on each tortilla, and roll up. Place the rolled tortillas, seam-side down, in single layer in the prepared baking dish.

4. In a medium bowl, combine the salsa and beans. Spoon the mixture over the enchiladas. Sprinkle the top with cheese.

5. Bake 20 minutes in the preheated oven, or until bubbly and lightly browned.

Chicken Enchiladas IV

Submitted by: **Doreen**

Makes: 4 servings
Preparation: 15 minutes
Cooking: 20 minutes
Ready In: 35 minutes

"A yummy recipe for chicken enchiladas."

INGREDIENTS

4 cooked skinless, boneless chicken breast halves

1 cup sour cream

2 cups shredded Cheddar cheese

4 green onions, chopped

1 tablespoon ground cumin

¼ cup chopped fresh cilantro

salt and pepper to taste

1 (12 ounce) package corn tortillas

1 (8 ounce) jar salsa

DIRECTIONS

1. Preheat oven to 350°F (175°C).

2. Shred the cooked chicken breast meat, and place in a large bowl. Mix in sour cream, shredded cheese, and green onions. Season with cumin, cilantro, salt, and pepper. Place a heaping spoonful of the mixture in each tortilla, roll up, and place rolled tortillas seam-side down in a 9x13 inch baking dish. Pour salsa over all.

3. Bake for about 20 minutes, or until heated through.

Broccoli, Rice, Cheese, and Chicken Casserole

Makes: 8 servings

Preparation: 15 minutes

Cooking: 30 minutes

Ready In: 45 minutes

Submitted by: **Heather**

"This is a delicious twist to broccoli, rice, and cheese casserole, and is VERY easy to make. You can also cut this in half. I use the 1 can cream of mushroom soup when I make half. You can also leave out the onion. It just gives it a little added flavor, but is still very good without it."

INGREDIENTS

2 cups water

2 cups uncooked instant rice

2 (10 ounce) cans chunk chicken, drained

1 (10.75 ounce) can condensed cream of mushroom soup

1 (10.75 ounce) can condensed cream of chicken soup

¼ cup butter

1 cup milk

1 (16 ounce) package frozen chopped broccoli

1 small white onion, chopped

1 pound processed cheese food

DIRECTIONS

1. Preheat oven to 350°F (175°C).

2. In a medium saucepan, bring the water to a boil. Mix in the instant rice, cover, and remove from heat. Let stand 5 minutes.

3. In a 9x13 inch baking dish, mix the prepared rice, chicken, cream of mushroom soup, cream of chicken soup, butter, milk, broccoli, onion, and processed cheese.

4. Bake in the preheated oven for 30 to 35 minutes, or until cheese is melted. Stir halfway through cooking to help cheese melt evenly.

Chicken Tetrazzini IV

Submitted by: **Mary**

Makes: 4 servings

Preparation: 15 minutes

Cooking: 45 minutes

Ready In: 1 hour

"Chicken, mushrooms and spaghetti baked in a rich, creamy white sauce flavored with Parmesan cheese and sherry."

INGREDIENTS

1 (8 ounce) package spaghetti, broken into pieces

¼ cup butter

¼ cup all-purpose flour

¾ teaspoon salt

¼ teaspoon ground black pepper

1 cup chicken broth

1 cup heavy cream

2 tablespoons sherry

1 (4.5 ounce) can sliced mushrooms, drained

2 cups chopped cooked chicken

½ cup grated Parmesan cheese

DIRECTIONS

1. Preheat oven to 350°F (175°C). Lightly grease a 9x13 inch baking dish.

2. Bring a large pot of lightly salted water to a boil. Add spaghetti, and cook for 8 to 10 minutes, or until al dente; drain.

3. Meanwhile, in a large saucepan, melt butter over low heat. Stir in flour, salt, and pepper. Cook, stirring, until smooth. Remove from heat, and gradually stir in chicken broth and cream.

4. Return to heat, and bring to a low boil for 1 minute, stirring constantly. Add sherry, then stir in cooked spaghetti, mushrooms, and chicken. Pour mixture into the prepared baking dish, and top with Parmesan cheese.

5. Bake 30 minutes in the preheated oven, until bubbly and lightly browned.

Quick Chicken Divan

Submitted by: **Shannon Fountain**

Makes: 8 servings

Preparation: 5 minutes

Cooking: 40 minutes

Ready In: 45 minutes

"My family loves this recipe. My kids love it because the broccoli is 'hidden' under all the chicken and cheese! This is an excellent way to use up leftovers."

INGREDIENTS

2 (10 ounce) packages frozen chopped broccoli

2 cooked boneless chicken breast halves, chopped

1 (10.75 ounce) can condensed cream of chicken soup

1 (10.75 ounce) can condensed cream of mushroom soup

½ cup mayonnaise

1 teaspoon lemon juice

1½ cups shredded Cheddar cheese

DIRECTIONS

1. Preheat oven to 350°F (175°C).

2. Place broccoli in the bottom of a 9x13 inch baking dish. Top with the chicken.

3. In a small bowl, blend the cream of chicken soup, cream of mushroom soup, mayonnaise, and lemon juice. Pour the mixture over the chicken. Top with Cheddar cheese.

4. Bake 35 to 40 minutes in the preheated oven, until bubbly and lightly browned.

Stuffed Acorn Squash Supreme

Submitted by: **Patrice Gerard**

Makes: 4 servings

Preparation: 10 minutes

Cooking: 20 minutes

Ready In: 30 minutes

"Acorn squash is partially cooked in the microwave, then filled with turkey sausage, broccoli, cheese, rice, and apples."

INGREDIENTS

1 (6 ounce) package broccoli and cheese flavored rice mix

1 pound turkey breakfast sausage

1 medium acorn squash, halved and seeded

1/2 cup chopped apple

2 teaspoons crushed coriander seed

1/2 cup shredded Monterey Jack cheese

DIRECTIONS

1. Prepare rice mix according to package directions; cover, and set aside.

2. Place squash halves cut side down onto a plate. Cook the squash in a microwave oven for 5 minutes on High, until tender but firm.

3. In a medium skillet over medium heat, cook sausage until evenly browned; drain, and set aside.

4. In a large bowl, mix together the prepared rice, sausage, apple, and coriander. Stuff each squash half with the mixture.

5. Cover stuffed squash halves with plastic wrap, and heat in the microwave until squash is cooked through and soft, about 5 minutes. Remove plastic, and top stuffed squash with cheese. Continue to cook until cheese is melted, about 1 minute.

Chicken Chimi in the Oven

Submitted by: **Jeri**

Makes: 6 servings

Preparation: 25 minutes

Cooking: 25 minutes

Ready In: 50 minutes

"A fragrant, spicy chicken mixture is rolled up in flour tortillas and baked. This is my absolute favorite recipe! Serve with salsa, sour cream, and guacamole."

INGREDIENTS

4 tablespoons olive oil, divided

1/2 cup chopped onion

2 cloves garlic, minced

2 cups salsa

3 tablespoons water

1/4 cup chili powder

1/2 teaspoon ground cumin

1/2 teaspoon ground cinnamon

1 pound cooked, shredded chicken breast meat

1 cup refried beans

6 (10 inch) flour tortillas

DIRECTIONS

1. Preheat oven to 425°F (220°C). Lightly grease a medium baking dish.

2. Heat 2 tablespoons oil in a large saucepan over medium heat. Sauté onion and garlic in oil until tender. Stir in salsa and water. Season with chili powder, cumin, and cinnamon. Transfer the mixture to a blender or food processor, and blend until smooth. Return mixture to the saucepan, stir in the chicken, and cook until heated through.

3. Spoon an equal amount of refried beans down center of each tortilla, and top with equal amounts of the chicken mixture. Fold tortillas over the filling, and secure with toothpicks. Arrange seam-side down in the prepared baking dish, and brush with the remaining olive oil.

4. Bake 15 minutes in the preheated oven, turning every 5 minutes, until golden brown and crisp.

BBQ Chicken Pizza

Submitted by: **Kimi Rae**

Makes: 1 - 12 inch pizza
Preparation: 30 minutes
Cooking: 15 minutes
Ready In: 45 minutes

"A topping of spicy barbeque sauce, diced chicken, cilantro, peppers, and onion all covered with cheese, and baked to bubbly goodness! This is similar to a recipe I had at a popular pizza place in California. My family LOVES it!"

INGREDIENTS

1 (12 inch) pre-baked pizza crust

1 cup spicy barbeque sauce

2 skinless boneless chicken breast halves, cooked and cubed

½ cup chopped fresh cilantro

1 cup sliced pepperoncini peppers

1 cup chopped red onion

2 cups shredded Colby-Monterey Jack cheese

DIRECTIONS

1. Preheat oven to 350°F (175°C).

2. Place pizza crust on a medium baking sheet. Spread the crust with barbeque sauce. Top with chicken, cilantro, pepperoncini peppers, onion, and cheese.

3. Bake in the preheated oven for 15 minutes, or until cheese is melted and bubbly.

Chicken Tacos

Submitted by: **Tara G.**

Makes: 8 servings

Preparation: 20 minutes

Cooking: 20 minutes

Ready In: 40 minutes

"This recipe is quick and easy - good for those nights you don't have a lot of time for dinner preparations."

INGREDIENTS

1 pound skinless, boneless chicken breast halves, cut into bite size pieces

1 cup lemonade

2 tablespoons olive oil

1 tablespoon lime juice

1½ teaspoons Worcestershire sauce

½ teaspoon garlic powder

½ teaspoon onion powder

1 bay leaf

1 (12 ounce) package corn tortillas

1 head lettuce, shredded

2 large tomatoes, chopped

1 (8 ounce) package shredded sharp Cheddar cheese

1 (8 ounce) jar salsa

1 (8 ounce) container sour cream

DIRECTIONS

1. In a large skillet over medium heat, combine chicken, lemonade, olive oil, lime juice, and Worcestershire sauce. Season with garlic powder, onion powder, and bay leaf. Simmer until chicken is no longer pink, and juices run clear, 15 to 20 minutes.

2. Meanwhile, warm the tortillas in the oven or microwave until soft. When chicken is fully cooked, transfer to serving bowl. Place lettuce, tomatoes, cheese, salsa, and sour cream in serving dishes. Each person can create their own wrap, using their preferred ingredients.

Goat Cheese and Spinach Turkey Burgers

Makes: 4 servings

Preparation: 10 minutes

Cooking: 15 minutes

Ready In: 25 minutes

Submitted by: **Nicole**

"This fast and easy recipe is perfect to make after a long day at work. The goat cheese adds a creamy flavor to sometimes bland turkey burgers. Served with a side salad, it makes a perfectly delicious meal."

INGREDIENTS

1½ pounds ground turkey breast

1 cup frozen chopped spinach, thawed
and drained

2 tablespoons goat cheese, crumbled

DIRECTIONS

1. Preheat the oven broiler.

2. In a medium bowl, mix ground turkey, spinach, and goat cheese. Form the mixture into 4 patties.

3. Arrange patties on a broiler pan, and place in the center of the preheated oven 15 minutes, or until cooked to desired doneness.

Amy's Triple Decker Turkey Bacon Sandwich

Submitted by: **Amy**

Makes: 1 serving

Preparation: 5 minutes

Cooking: 2 minutes

Ready In: 7 minutes

"Layers of turkey bacon, Cheddar cheese, lettuce, tomato, and mayo grace two slices of bread for this triple decker doozie. A wonderful sandwich at any time of the day."

INGREDIENTS

2 slices white bread

¼ cup mayonnaise

3 lettuce leaves

1 tomato, thinly sliced

3 slices turkey bacon

3 slices Cheddar cheese

DIRECTIONS

1. Toast the bread slices.

2. Spread a thin layer of mayonnaise on each slice. Layer bottom slice with lettuce, tomato, turkey bacon, and cheese. Spread another thin layer of mayonnaise on the cheese; repeat layers twice. Top with second slice of bread. Heat in microwave for 45 seconds to 1 minute, or until cheese is melted.

Cuban Midnight Sandwich

Submitted by: **Maruchy Ramos-Lachance**

Makes: 4 sandwiches

Preparation: 20 minutes

Cooking: 5 minutes

Ready In: 25 minutes

"This sandwich is called a 'Media Noche' which translates to 'Midnight.' It makes a wonderful dinner sandwich because it is served hot. A nice side dish is black bean soup or black beans and rice, and plantain chips."

INGREDIENTS

1 cup mayonnaise

5 tablespoons Italian dressing

4 hoagie rolls, split lengthwise

4 tablespoons prepared mustard

1/2 pound thinly sliced deli turkey meat

1/2 pound thinly sliced cooked ham

1/2 pound thinly sliced Swiss cheese

1 cup dill pickle slices

1/2 cup olive oil

DIRECTIONS

1. In a small bowl, mix together mayonnaise and Italian dressing. Spread mixture on hoagie rolls. Spread each roll with mustard. On each roll, arrange layers of turkey, ham, and cheese. Top each with dill pickle slices. Close sandwiches, and brush tops and bottoms with olive oil.

2. Heat a non-stick skillet over medium high heat. Place sandwiches in skillet. Cook sandwiches for 2 minutes, pressing down with a plate covered with aluminum foil. Flip, and cook for 2 more minutes, or until cheese is melted. Remove from heat, place on plates, and cut in half diagonally.

beef and pork

Most supermarkets sell beef and pork that's already cut into bite-size strips (sometimes called "stir-fry" meat). It's usually the same price, and sometimes cheaper, than buying whole pieces of meat, and it will save you some prep time. If you cook with ground beef or bulk sausage fairly often, you can get the jump on dinner by sautéing a bunch of it at once, and then distributing meal-size portions into freezer containers. It will be ready when you are; just throw a handful into soup, chili, pasta sauce, stroganoff, sloppy joes, tacos and more!

Broccoli Beef

Submitted by: **Sara**

Makes: 4 servings

Preparation: 15 minutes

Cooking: 15 minutes

Ready In: 30 minutes

"Round steak and broccoli are quickly cooked in a soy ginger sauce. Serve over hot over rice or noodles."

INGREDIENTS

¼ cup all-purpose flour

1 (10.5 ounce) can beef broth

2 tablespoons white sugar

2 tablespoons soy sauce

1 pound boneless round steak, cut into bite size pieces

¼ teaspoon chopped fresh ginger root

1 clove garlic, minced

4 cups chopped fresh broccoli

DIRECTIONS

1. In a small bowl, combine flour, broth, sugar, and soy sauce. Stir until sugar and flour are dissolved.

2. In a large skillet or wok over high heat, cook and stir beef 2 to 4 minutes, or until browned. Stir in broth mixture, ginger, garlic, and broccoli. Bring to a boil, then reduce heat. Simmer 5 to 10 minutes, or until sauce thickens.

Mongolian Beef

Submitted by: **Onemina**

Makes: 6 servings

Preparation: 35 minutes

Cooking: 10 minutes

Ready In: 45 minutes

"A simple but spicy dish with beef, carrots and green onions. Serve over rice for a very filling meal."

INGREDIENTS

1 teaspoon sesame seeds

1 tablespoon soy sauce

1 tablespoon cornstarch

2 cloves garlic, minced

1 pound beef round steak, cut into thin strips

3/4 cup water

2 tablespoons soy sauce

2 1/2 teaspoons cornstarch

1/2 teaspoon white sugar

1 teaspoon red pepper flakes

2 tablespoons vegetable oil, divided

2 carrots, thinly sliced

1 bunch green onions, cut into 2 inch pieces

DIRECTIONS

1. In a dry skillet over medium heat, toast sesame seeds for 1 to 2 minutes, or until the seeds begin to turn golden brown; set aside.

2. In a medium bowl, mix together 1 tablespoon soy sauce, 1 tablespoon cornstarch, and minced garlic. Stir in beef strips. Let stand for at least 10 minutes.

3. In a separate small bowl, mix together water, 2 tablespoons soy sauce, 2½ teaspoons cornstarch, sugar, sesame seeds, and red pepper flakes; set aside.

4. Heat 1 tablespoon of oil in a wok or skillet over high heat. Cook and stir beef in hot oil for 1 minute; remove, and set aside. Heat remaining tablespoon of oil in the same pan. Sauté carrots and white part of green onions for 2 minutes. Stir in green parts of the green onion, and sauté for 1 minute. Stir in sesame seed mixture and beef. Cook and stir until sauce boils and thickens.

Sukiyaki

Submitted by: **Sara**

Makes: 6 servings
Preparation: 10 minutes
Cooking: 20 minutes
Ready In: 30 minutes

"Serve this simple Japanese dish over thin Japanese noodles or rice, if desired."

INGREDIENTS

1 tablespoon oil for frying

1½ pounds beef sirloin strips

²/₃ cup soy sauce

2 teaspoons monosodium glutamate (MSG)

¹/₃ cup chicken broth

¹/₃ cup white sugar

3 small onions, sliced

2 cups chopped celery

1 (14 ounce) can bamboo shoots, drained and chopped

4 green onions, sliced

1 (4.5 ounce) can mushrooms, drained

1 (8 ounce) can water chestnuts, drained

1 teaspoon cornstarch

DIRECTIONS

1. Heat oil in a large skillet or wok over medium-high heat. Brown beef in hot oil, then stir in soy sauce, MSG, broth, and sugar. Mix in onion and celery, and cook until tender. Stir in bamboo shoots, green onions, mushrooms, and water chestnuts. Reduce heat to medium, stir in cornstarch, and simmer until sauce is thickened.

Veal Forestiere

Submitted by: **Bobbi**

Makes: 6 servings

Preparation: 15 minutes

Cooking: 15 minutes

Ready In: 30 minutes

"Breaded veal cutlets with a Marsala mushroom sauce - delicious!"

INGREDIENTS

1½ pounds thin veal cutlets

¼ cup all-purpose flour for coating

3 tablespoons butter

1 tablespoon minced garlic

1 tablespoon minced shallot

½ pound crimini mushrooms, sliced

½ cup Marsala wine

½ cup veal stock

1 (10 ounce) can artichoke hearts, drained and sliced

salt and pepper to taste

DIRECTIONS

1. Lightly flour veal cutlets, and shake off the excess. Melt butter in a large skillet over medium-high heat. Place cutlets in pan, and cook 1 to 2 minutes per side, until browned and nearly cooked through. Remove veal from pan, and set aside.

2. Sauté garlic and shallots in skillet until shallots are tender. Stir in mushrooms, and continue to cook until mushrooms begin to sweat. Pour in the wine; cook 2 to 3 minutes more, stirring with a spoon to scrape the bottom of the pan. Pour in stock, and simmer 5 to 10 minutes, or until liquid begins to reduce.

3. Return veal to pan with artichokes, and cook until heated through. Season with salt and pepper. To serve, arrange the veal on plates, and spoon the sauce over.

Steak Parmesan

Submitted by: **Mary Lynn**

Makes: 8 servings

Preparation: 15 minutes

Cooking: 40 minutes

Ready In: 55 minutes

"Here's a fairly simple recipe for something different to do with cubed steak. It involves breading meat with bread crumbs and grated Parmesan cheese, then combining it with your favorite spaghetti sauce. Serve over pasta with additional cheese. A real family pleaser!"

INGREDIENTS

1 cup dry bread crumbs

1/2 cup grated Parmesan cheese

salt and pepper to taste

2 pounds cube steak

1/4 cup vegetable oil for frying

1 (32 ounce) jar spaghetti sauce

DIRECTIONS

1. In a medium bowl, combine the bread crumbs, Parmesan cheese, salt, and pepper. Dredge the meat in the crumbs.

2. Heat oil in a large skillet over medium-high heat. Place the breaded meat in the oil, and sauté for 5 to 10 minutes, or until well browned on both sides.

3. Drain excess oil, and pour in the spaghetti sauce. Reduce heat to low, and simmer for 30 minutes.

Sirloin Steak with Garlic Butter

Submitted by: **Solana**

Makes: 8 servings

Preparation: 20 minutes

Cooking: 10 minutes

Ready In: 30 minutes

"I have never tasted any other steak that came even close to the ones made with this recipe. If you are having steak, don't skimp on flavor to save a few calories. The butter makes this steak melt in your mouth wonderful."

INGREDIENTS

½ cup butter

2 teaspoons garlic powder

4 cloves garlic, minced

4 pounds beef top sirloin steaks

salt and pepper to taste

DIRECTIONS

1. Preheat an outdoor grill for high heat.

2. In a small saucepan, melt butter over medium-low heat with garlic powder and minced garlic. Set aside.

3. Sprinkle both sides of each steak with salt and pepper.

4. Grill steaks 4 to 5 minutes per side, or to desired doneness. When done, transfer to warmed plates. Brush tops liberally with garlic butter, and allow to rest for 2 to 3 minutes before serving.

Filet Mignon with Rich Balsamic Glaze

Submitted by: **Linda W.**

Makes: 2 servings

Preparation: 5 minutes

Cooking: 15 minutes

Ready In: 20 minutes

"This is an elegant and quick romantic dinner for two. Wonderful served with steamed asparagus and baby red potatoes."

INGREDIENTS

2 (4 ounce) beef tenderloin steaks

½ teaspoon freshly ground black pepper to taste

salt to taste

¼ cup balsamic vinegar

¼ cup dry red wine

DIRECTIONS

1. Sprinkle freshly ground pepper over both sides of each steak, and sprinkle with salt to taste.

2. Heat a nonstick skillet over medium-high heat. Place steaks in hot pan, and cook for 1 minute on each side, or until browned. Reduce heat to medium-low, and add balsamic vinegar and red wine. Cover, and cook for 4 minutes on each side, basting with sauce when you turn the meat over.

3. Remove steaks to two warmed plates, spoon one tablespoon of glaze over each, and serve immediately.

Steak Diane

Submitted by: **Sallie**

Makes: 4 servings
Preparation: 20 minutes
Cooking: 20 minutes
Ready In: 40 minutes

"This recipe of strip steak pounded thin, seasoned with dry mustard, and pan fried, goes great with cooked mushrooms. Just add them to the pan during the last few minutes of cooking time."

INGREDIENTS

4 (1/2 pound) strip steaks, cut ½ inch thick

salt to taste

freshly ground black pepper to taste

1 teaspoon dry mustard, divided

¼ cup margarine

3 tablespoons lemon juice

2 teaspoons minced fresh chives

1 teaspoon Worcestershire sauce

DIRECTIONS

1. Pound steaks to be ¼ inch thick, and sprinkle each side with salt, black pepper, and 1/8 teaspoon mustard; rub into the meat.

2. Melt margarine in a large skillet over medium-high heat. Fry 2 of the steaks for 2 minutes on each side, and transfer to a hot serving plate. Repeat with remaining 2 steaks.

3. Add lemon juice, chives, Worcestershire sauce, and remaining mustard to the pan, and bring to a boil. Return the steaks to the pan to heat through, and coat with sauce.

Country Fried Steak and Milk Gravy

Submitted by: **Patti**

Makes: 4 servings

Preparation: 15 minutes

Cooking: 20 minutes

Ready In: 35 minutes

"I have been making this for years and my family just loves it. The gravy is great served over the steak, or on mashed potatoes."

INGREDIENTS

4 (4 ounce) cube steaks

1/2 teaspoon salt, divided

1 3/4 teaspoons ground black pepper, divided

1 cup all-purpose flour

2 eggs, lightly beaten

1/4 cup lard

1 cup milk

DIRECTIONS

1. Season meat with 1/4 teaspoon of the salt and 1/4 teaspoon of the pepper; set aside. In a shallow dish, mix flour with 1 teaspoon of the pepper. Dredge each steak in flour. Dip in beaten egg, then dredge in flour again.

2. Heat lard in a large, heavy skillet over medium-high heat. Fry steaks 3 to 4 minutes on each side, or until golden brown. Drain on paper towels.

3. Pour off all but 2 tablespoons of the fat. Sprinkle 2 tablespoons of the dredging flour into oil. Cook over medium heat for 1 minute, scraping up any browned bits from the bottom of skillet. Gradually whisk in milk. Cook, stirring frequently, 3 to 4 minutes, or until thickened and bubbly. Add 1/4 teaspoon salt, and 1/4 to 1/2 teaspoon pepper; gravy should be quite peppery.

Philly Steak Sandwich

Submitted by: **Wendy L**

Makes: 4 servings

Preparation: 15 minutes

Cooking: 25 minutes

Ready In: 40 minutes

"These sandwiches are delicious. I purchase steak that has been sliced for making stir-fry, which takes a little less time, but achieves the same results."

INGREDIENTS

1 pound beef sirloin, cut into thin 2 inch strips

1/2 teaspoon salt

1/2 teaspoon black pepper

1/2 teaspoon paprika

1/2 teaspoon chili powder

1/2 teaspoon onion powder

1/2 teaspoon garlic powder

1/2 teaspoon dried thyme

1/2 teaspoon dried marjoram

1/2 teaspoon dried basil

3 tablespoons vegetable oil

1 onion, sliced

1 green bell pepper, julienned

3 ounces Swiss cheese, thinly sliced

4 hoagie rolls, split lengthwise

DIRECTIONS

1. Place the beef in a large bowl. In a small bowl, mix together salt, pepper, paprika, chili powder, onion powder, garlic powder, thyme, marjoram and basil. Sprinkle over beef.

2. Heat half of the oil in a skillet over medium-high heat. Sauté beef to desired doneness, and remove from pan. Heat the remaining oil in the skillet, and sauté the onion and green pepper.

3. Preheat oven on broiler setting.

4. Divide the meat between the bottoms of 4 rolls, layer with onion and green pepper, then top with sliced cheese. Place on cookie sheet, and broil until cheese is melted. Cover with tops of rolls, and serve.

Sauerbraten Klopse (Sauerbraten Meatballs)

Makes: 4 servings
Preparation: 15 minutes
Cooking: 45 minutes
Ready In: 1 hour

Submitted by: **Christine Johnson**

"Beef meatballs seasoned with cloves and allspice. Pan fried, and smothered in gravy."

INGREDIENTS

1 pound lean ground beef

1/4 cup milk

1/4 cup dry bread crumbs

1/8 teaspoon ground cloves

1/8 teaspoon ground allspice

1/2 teaspoon salt

1/2 teaspoon ground black pepper

2 tablespoons vegetable oil

1 cup water

1/2 cup distilled white vinegar

4 tablespoons packed brown sugar

3/4 teaspoon ground ginger

1 bay leaf

2 tablespoons all-purpose flour

2 tablespoons water

DIRECTIONS

1. In a large bowl, mix together ground beef, milk, and bread crumbs. Season with cloves, allspice, salt, and pepper. Shape into 1 inch balls.

2. Heat oil in a large heavy skillet over medium heat. Cook the meatballs until evenly brown; drain excess fat. Stir in water, vinegar, brown sugar, ginger, and bay leaf. Cover, and simmer for 30 minutes. Skim off any fat. Transfer meatballs to a serving dish, and keep warm.

3. Combine flour with 2 tablespoons of water, and whisk into pan. Cook, stirring constantly, until thickened. Pour gravy over meatballs.

allrecipes tried & true quick and easy | beef and pork

Sweet and Sour Meatballs IV

Submitted by: **Rachel**

Makes: 6 servings

Preparation: 20 minutes

Cooking: 40 minutes

Ready In: 1 hour

"These flavor packed meatballs are easy to make, and sure to be a hit with your family! Serve them over rice."

INGREDIENTS

5 teaspoons beef bouillon granules, divided

¼ cup boiling water

1½ pounds lean ground beef

1 cup dry bread crumbs

¾ cup minced onion

1 egg

1 (20 ounce) can pineapple chunks, drained with juice reserved

⅓ cup fresh lemon juice

3 tablespoons packed brown sugar

2 tablespoons soy sauce

1 teaspoon grated fresh ginger root

2 tablespoons cornstarch

1 green bell pepper, chopped

DIRECTIONS

1. In a small saucepan, dissolve 2 teaspoons of the bouillon granules in ¼ cup boiling water. In a large bowl, combine ground beef, bread crumbs, onion, and egg. Mix in the dissolved bouillon. Shape into meatballs, about 1 to 2 inches in diameter.

2. In a large saucepan over medium heat, brown the meatballs on all sides. In a small bowl, combine ¼ cup of the reserved pineapple juice, lemon juice, brown sugar, soy sauce, remaining beef bouillon granules, and ginger. Pour into the pan with meatballs. Cover, and simmer for 25 minutes.

3. In a small bowl, combine remaining pineapple juice and cornstarch. Stir into meatball mixture, and simmer until thickened. Add green pepper and pineapple chunks; heat thoroughly.

Green Bean Okazu

Submitted by: **April Hilton**

Makes: 4 servings

Preparation: 10 minutes

Cooking: 30 minutes

Ready In: 40 minutes

"This was my favorite dinner growing up. It's a quick and easy way to get picky kids to eat green beans, because of the sweet sauce. It's great served over rice, or alone."

INGREDIENTS

1 pound ground beef

1 pound green beans, trimmed and cut into 1 inch pieces

1 cup water

¼ cup white sugar

¼ cup soy sauce

DIRECTIONS

1. In a large skillet over medium heat, cook the ground beef until evenly brown; drain excess fat.

2. Stir in green beans and about 1 cup water. Cover, and cook until beans are tender, 15 to 20 minutes.

3. Season with sugar and soy sauce, and cook uncovered for 5 minutes.

Sloppy Joes II

Submitted by: **Tamara**

Makes: 6 servings

Preparation: 10 minutes

Cooking: 30 minutes

Ready In: 40 minutes

"This is the recipe my mother used for sloppy joes, and it always gets compliments!"

INGREDIENTS

1 pound lean ground beef

1/4 cup chopped onion

1/4 cup chopped green bell pepper

1/2 teaspoon garlic powder

1 teaspoon prepared yellow mustard

3/4 cup ketchup

3 teaspoons brown sugar

salt to taste

ground black pepper to taste

DIRECTIONS

1. In a medium skillet over medium heat, brown the ground beef, onion, and green pepper; drain off liquids.

2. Stir in the garlic powder, mustard, ketchup, and brown sugar; mix thoroughly. Reduce heat, and simmer for 30 minutes. Season with salt and pepper.

Barbequed Hamburgers

Submitted by: **Paula**

Makes: 8 servings

Preparation: 20 minutes

Cooking: 25 minutes

Ready In: 45 minutes

"This is an heirloom recipe from my grandmother. We used to beg my mom to make these. Not intended to be placed on a grill, they are best served over rice with a nice green salad."

INGREDIENTS

1 pound ground beef

1/2 cup uncooked rolled oats

2/3 cup evaporated milk

2 tablespoons minced onion

1/8 teaspoon salt

1/8 teaspoon ground black pepper

4 teaspoons Worcestershire sauce

2 tablespoons vinegar

4 teaspoons granulated sugar

2/3 cup ketchup

1/4 cup chopped onion

3 tablespoons vegetable oil

DIRECTIONS

1. In a medium bowl, mix the ground beef, oats, milk, 2 tablespoons minced onion, salt, and pepper. Let stand for a few minutes until milk is absorbed, and shape into 8 patties.

2. In a small bowl, thoroughly mix the Worcestershire sauce, vinegar, sugar, ketchup, and 1/4 cup chopped onion; set aside.

3. Heat the oil in a medium skillet over medium heat, and fry the patties until brown on both sides. Pour the sauce in with the patties, and reduce heat. Continue cooking about 15 minutes.

Firecracker Burgers

Submitted by: **Gail**

Makes: 4 servings

Preparation: 10 minutes

Cooking: 20 minutes

Ready In: 30 minutes

"This is a great, easy burger recipe. The ground beef is combined with green chile peppers and beef bouillon. This makes them very moist and flavorful. Serve on hamburger buns with your favorite fixings."

INGREDIENTS

1 pound ground beef

1 (4 ounce) can diced green chilies, drained

1 teaspoon beef bouillon granules

4 slices Monterey Jack cheese

DIRECTIONS

1. Preheat an outdoor grill for high heat, and lightly oil grate.

2. In a medium bowl, mix the beef, diced green chilies, and bouillon. Shape into 4 patties.

3. Grill patties 3 to 8 minutes per side, or to desired doneness. Top each patty with cheese about 2 minutes prior to removing from grill.

Cajun Style Burgers

Submitted by: **Gail**

Makes: 4 servings

Preparation: 10 minutes

Cooking: 20 minutes

Ready In: 30 minutes

"These are spicy burgers cooked on the grill, and topped with a hot barbeque sauce. Serve with hamburger rolls, lettuce, tomato, and red onion."

INGREDIENTS

1 pound ground beef

3 tablespoons dry bread crumbs

1 egg

3 green onions, chopped

1 tablespoon Cajun seasoning

1 tablespoon prepared mustard

¼ cup barbecue sauce

1 teaspoon Cajun seasoning

4 slices Cheddar cheese

DIRECTIONS

1. Preheat an outdoor grill for high heat, and lightly oil grate.

2. In a medium bowl, mix the ground beef, bread crumbs, egg, green onions, 1 tablespoon Cajun seasoning, and mustard. Form into 4 patties.

3. In a small bowl, blend the barbeque sauce and 1 teaspoon Cajun seasoning.

4. Cook the patties on the prepared grill to desired doneness. Place a slice of cheese on each burger, and allow to melt. Serve with seasoned barbecue sauce.

Barbecue Beef Cups

Submitted by: **Karen**

Makes: 6 servings

Preparation: 15 minutes

Cooking: 25 minutes

Ready In: 40 minutes

"This is a quick and easy recipe given to me by a friend. My family loves it."

INGREDIENTS

¾ pound ground beef

½ cup barbeque sauce

1 tablespoon dried minced onion

1 (12 ounce) package refrigerated biscuit dough

⅓ cup shredded Cheddar cheese

DIRECTIONS

1. Preheat oven to 350°F (175°C). Grease the cups of a muffin pan.

2. In a large heavy skillet over medium heat, cook beef until evenly brown. Drain excess fat. Stir in barbeque sauce and dried onion. Simmer for a few minutes over low heat.

3. Flatten each biscuit, and press into cups of the prepared muffin pan. Make sure the dough comes to the top of the pan. Spoon a portion of the meat mixture into each dough cup.

4. Bake in preheated oven for 12 minutes. Sprinkle with cheese, and bake for 3 more minutes.

Beef and Mushroom Stuffed Peppers

Submitted by: **Bob Tipton**

Makes: 3 servings

Preparation: 20 minutes

Cooking: 30 minutes

Ready In: 50 minutes

"A beefy alternative to 'Italian-style' stuffed peppers, great with any white rice-based side dish, or mashed potatoes."

INGREDIENTS

1 pound ground beef

1 cup fresh mushrooms, sliced

1/2 white onion, diced

2 cups beef gravy

salt and pepper to taste

3 small red bell peppers, halved and seeded

3/4 cup shredded Monterey Jack cheese

DIRECTIONS

1. Preheat oven to 375 °F (190°C).

2. Brown beef in a large skillet over medium-high heat. Halfway through browning, add mushrooms and onion. Continue cooking until meat is fully browned; drain fat from skillet. Stir in enough gravy to bond mixture without making it soupy. Season with salt and pepper, and set aside.

3. Meanwhile, heat a medium saucepan of water until boiling. Place peppers in water, and boil for 2 to 3 minutes, until just tender; remove from water. Place peppers, hollow side up, in a 9x13 inch baking dish, and fill each with beef mixture.

4. Bake in preheated oven for 15 to 20 minutes, until bubbling. Top with cheese, and bake for an additional 5 to 10 minutes. Serve in a small pool of gravy.

Enchiladas

Submitted by: **Vanessa Robbins**

Makes: 6 servings

Preparation: 15 minutes

Cooking: 40 minutes

Ready In: 55 minutes

"These are beef-filled tortilla shells baked in a creamy chicken soup and cheese sauce. My husband absolutely loves these. I served them to guests once with Mexican rice, and they went home with the recipe. Enjoy!"

INGREDIENTS

1½ pounds lean ground beef

1 bunch green onions, finely chopped

1 diced fresh jalapeno pepper, or to taste

¼ cup water

1 (1.25 ounce) package taco seasoning mix

1 cup plain yogurt

1 (10.75 ounce) can condensed cream of chicken soup

2 cups shredded mozzarella cheese

6 (6 inch) corn tortillas

DIRECTIONS

1. Preheat oven to 350°F (175°C).

2. In a large skillet over medium heat, cook the ground beef, green onion, and jalapeno pepper until the beef is evenly brown. Stir in water and taco seasoning. Simmer until water has evaporated.

3. In a medium bowl, mix together yogurt, condensed soup, and cheese.

4. Divide the meat mixture evenly between tortillas. Place a couple of tablespoons of cheese mixture over meat, and roll up. Place in a 7x11 inch baking dish. Repeat for each tortilla. Spoon remaining cheese mixture over the top of the tortillas.

5. Bake in preheated oven for 20 to 30 minutes.

Taco Pies

Submitted by: **Carole**

Makes: 8 servings

Preparation: 15 minutes

Cooking: 25 minutes

Ready In: 40 minutes

"This is an easy, quick recipe using hamburger."

INGREDIENTS

2 (9 inch) deep dish frozen pie crusts, thawed

1 pound ground beef

1 (16 ounce) can refried beans

1 onion, chopped

1 cup crushed tortilla chips

1 cup shredded Cheddar cheese

2 cups shredded lettuce

1 large tomato, diced

sour cream

black olives

DIRECTIONS

1. Preheat oven to 350°F (175°C). Bake pie crusts following package directions, but cutting the bake time in half.

2. In a large, heavy skillet over medium-high heat, cook the ground beef until evenly brown; drain excess fat.

3. Place half the refried beans in each pie shell, smearing over the bottom and the sides of the partially baked shells. Spread a layer of ground meat over the beans, and top with the onion, crushed tortilla chips, and cheese.

4. Bake 15 to 20 minutes, or until the crust is golden brown, and the cheese is bubbly. Top with lettuce, tomato, sour cream, and black olives.

Stir-Fry Pork with Ginger

Submitted by: **Jenny Au**

Makes: 2 servings

Preparation: 15 minutes

Cooking: 15 minutes

Ready In: 30 minutes

"A simple Chinese dish. The wine and ginger gives the dish its fragrant smell. Best served with warm rice."

INGREDIENTS

2 tablespoons vegetable oil

1/2 inch piece fresh ginger, thinly sliced

1/4 pound thinly sliced lean pork

1 teaspoon soy sauce

1/2 teaspoon dark soy sauce

1/2 teaspoon salt

1/3 teaspoon sugar

1 teaspoon sesame oil

1 green onion, chopped

1 tablespoon Chinese rice wine

DIRECTIONS

1. Heat oil in a large skillet or wok over medium-high heat. Fry ginger in hot oil until fragrant, then add pork, soy sauce, dark soy sauce, salt, and sugar. Cook, stirring occasionally, for 10 minutes.

2. Stir in the sesame oil, green onion, and rice wine. Simmer until the pork is tender.

Spicy Peach-Glazed Pork Chops

Submitted by: **Virginia C.**

Makes: 4 servings

Preparation: 10 minutes

Cooking: 20 minutes

Ready In: 30 minutes

"Sweet and spicy boneless pork chops made with a special sauce that includes peach preserves and white wine. Serve with sweet potato latkes."

INGREDIENTS

1 cup peach preserves

1½ tablespoons Worcestershire sauce

½ teaspoon chile paste

4 boneless pork chops

1 teaspoon ground ginger

1 pinch ground cinnamon

salt and pepper to taste

2 tablespoons vegetable oil

½ cup white wine

DIRECTIONS

1. In a small bowl, mix together the peach preserves, Worcestershire sauce, and chile paste. Rinse pork chops, and pat dry. Sprinkle the chops with ginger, cinnamon, salt, and pepper.

2. Heat oil in a large skillet over medium-high heat. Sear the chops for about 2 minutes on each side. Remove from the pan, and set aside.

3. Pour white wine into the pan, and stir to scrape the bottom of the pan. Stir in the peach preserves mixture. Return the chops to the pan, and flip to coat with the sauce. Reduce heat to medium low, and cook the pork chops for about 8 minutes on each side, or until done.

Caramel Apple Pork Chops

Submitted by: **Karena**

Makes: 4 servings

Preparation: 20 minutes

Cooking: 10 minutes

Ready In: 45 minutes

"Warm, spicy, and sweet, this wonderful Fall recipe is a guaranteed favorite for kids, and is great with smashed potatoes and buttered green beans."

INGREDIENTS

4 (3/4 inch) thick pork chops

1 teaspoon vegetable oil

2 tablespoons brown sugar

salt and pepper to taste

1/8 teaspoon ground cinnamon

1/8 teaspoon ground nutmeg

2 tablespoons unsalted butter

2 tart apples - peeled, cored and sliced

3 tablespoons pecans (optional)

DIRECTIONS

1. Preheat oven to 175°F (80°C). Place a medium dish in the oven to warm.

2. Heat a large skillet over medium-high heat. Brush chops lightly with oil, and place in hot pan. Cook for 5 to 6 minutes, turning occasionally, or until done. Transfer to the warm dish, and keep warm in the preheated oven.

3. In a small bowl, combine brown sugar, salt, pepper, cinnamon, and nutmeg. Add butter to skillet, and stir in brown sugar mixture and apples. Cover, and cook for 3 to 4 minutes, or until apples are just tender. Remove apples with a slotted spoon, and arrange on top of chops. Keep warm in the preheated oven.

4. Continue cooking mixture uncovered in skillet, until sauce thickens slightly. Spoon sauce over apples and chops. Sprinkle with pecans.

Mushroom Pork Chops

Submitted by: **Melissa McGee**

Makes: 4 servings

Preparation: 5 minutes

Cooking: 35 minutes

Ready In: 40 minutes

"Quick and easy, but very delicious. One of my family's favorites served over brown rice."

INGREDIENTS

4 pork chops

salt and pepper to taste

1 pinch garlic salt, or to taste

1 onion, chopped

½ pound fresh mushrooms, sliced

1 (10.75 ounce) can condensed cream of mushroom soup

DIRECTIONS

1. Season pork chops with salt, pepper, and garlic salt to taste.

2. In a large skillet, brown the chops over medium-high heat. Add the onion and mushrooms, and sauté for one minute. Pour cream of mushroom soup over chops. Cover skillet, and reduce temperature to medium-low. Simmer 20 to 30 minutes, or until chops are cooked through.

Skillet Chops with Mushroom Gravy

Submitted by: **Kathy Statham**

Makes: 4 servings

Preparation: 10 minutes

Cooking: 30 minutes

Ready In: 40 minutes

"This is a very comforting, satisfying dish, and makes a great meal when served with rice or mashed potatoes and a tossed salad."

INGREDIENTS

½ cup dry bread crumbs

2 tablespoons grated Parmesan cheese

4 pork chops

1 tablespoon vegetable oil

1 (10.75 ounce) can condensed cream of mushroom soup

½ cup milk

DIRECTIONS

1. Combine bread crumbs and Parmesan cheese in a large resealable plastic bag. Add chops two at a time, and shake to coat.

2. Heat oil in a large skillet over medium-high heat, and cook chops until brown on both sides. Remove chops from skillet, and reduce heat to medium.

3. Blend soup and milk in the skillet, stirring to scrape up the bits of breading left over from the chops. You can adjust the amount of milk depending on how thick you want the gravy to be (it will thin a bit during the cooking process). Bring to a gentle boil, increasing heat slightly if necessary. When soup mixture is bubbling, return chops to skillet. Cover, and reduce heat to low. Simmer for 20 minutes, or until chops are cooked through.

Pork Tenderloin with Creamy Herb Sauce

Submitted by: **Carrie**

Makes: 6 servings

Preparation: 15 minutes

Cooking: 30 minutes

Ready In: 45 minutes

"A wonderfully elegant and easy pork tenderloin dish with a creamy herbed wine sauce. Very rich, without all of the fat and calories! Serve with garlic mashed potatoes. A wonderful dish."

INGREDIENTS

1 tablespoon vegetable oil

½ cup minced carrots

1½ pounds pork tenderloin medallions

2 teaspoons all-purpose flour

1 tablespoon dried basil

1 tablespoon dried parsley

½ teaspoon ground black pepper

½ teaspoon beef bouillon granules

⅔ cup light cream

¼ cup dry white wine

DIRECTIONS

1. Heat oil in a skillet over medium heat; cook carrots in oil for 5 minutes, stirring often. Add pork, and cook until lightly browned. Remove only pork, and keep warm.

2. In the skillet, stir together flour, basil, parsley, pepper, and beef granules. Whisk in light cream, stirring until thick. Stir in wine. Return pork to pan, reduce heat to low, and cover. Simmer for 20 minutes, stirring occasionally.

Sausage Gravy

Submitted by: **Rene**

Makes: 8 servings

Preparation: 5 minutes

Cooking: 25 minutes

Ready In: 30 minutes

"My mother learned how to make this while we lived in Nashville many years ago, and it is now a family favorite. Good old-fashioned sausage gravy. It's her most requested recipe from family and friends alike. Serve over biscuits or toast."

INGREDIENTS

1 pound ground pork sausage

3 tablespoons bacon grease

¼ cup all-purpose flour

3 cups milk

½ teaspoon salt

¼ teaspoon ground black pepper

DIRECTIONS

1. Brown sausage in a large skillet over medium-high heat. Set aside, leaving the drippings in the skillet.

2. Mix bacon grease into the sausage drippings. Reduce heat to medium, combine with flour, and stir constantly until mixture just turns golden brown.

3. Gradually whisk milk into skillet. When the mixture is smooth, thickened, and begins to bubble, return the sausage to skillet. Season with salt and pepper. Reduce heat, and simmer for about 15 minutes.

Italian Sausage and Zucchini

Submitted by: **Michelle W**

Makes: 6 servings

Preparation: 20 minutes

Cooking: 25 minutes

Ready In: 45 minutes

"This goes in the quick and easy category...and yummy too! Serve over cooked rice or pasta."

INGREDIENTS

1½ pounds Italian sausage links

2 small zucchini, sliced

1 small yellow squash, sliced

½ cup chopped onion

1 (14.5 ounce) can stewed tomatoes, with liquid

DIRECTIONS

1. In a large skillet over medium heat, brown the Italian sausage until the inside is no longer pink. Cut sausage into ¼ inch slices, and continue cooking until browned.

2. Stir in the zucchini, yellow squash, and onion; cook and stir for 2 minutes. Pour in the tomatoes, with liquid. Reduce heat, cover, and simmer for 10 to 15 minutes.

Bubble 'n' Squeak

Submitted by: **Doreen Friesen**

Makes: 6 servings

Preparation: 15 minutes

Cooking: 15 minutes

Ready In: 30 minutes

"Cabbage, bacon, ham, onion and leftover potatoes make up this tasty, easy dish. This is a great way to get the kids to eat cabbage. Using leftovers makes this main dish especially quick to make. I recommend using a good nonstick pan. Serve with ketchup, if desired."

INGREDIENTS

½ medium head cabbage, sliced

3 slices bacon, diced

1 onion, thinly sliced

1 cup cubed cooked ham

1 tablespoon butter

3 cups potatoes - baked, cooled and thinly sliced

½ teaspoon paprika

salt and pepper to taste

DIRECTIONS

1. In a medium saucepan, cook cabbage in a small amount of water for about 5 minutes, or until tender. Drain, and set aside.

2. In a well-seasoned cast iron skillet, cook bacon and onion until onion is soft and bacon is cooked. Add ham, and cook until heated through. Add butter, then mix in the cooked cabbage and potatoes. Season with paprika, salt, and pepper. Cook until browned on bottom, turn, and brown again.

Hoagie Bake

Submitted by: **Cindy**

Makes: 8 servings

Preparation: 15 minutes

Cooking: 35 minutes

Ready In: 50 minutes

"A great, fairly quick recipe for a delicious hoagie bake."

INGREDIENTS

2 (8 ounce) packages refrigerated crescent rolls

1/4 pound salami, sliced

1/4 pound cooked ham, sliced

1/4 pound pepperoni sausage, sliced

8 slices Provolone cheese

8 slices Swiss cheese

3 eggs, beaten

2 tablespoons grated Parmesan cheese

DIRECTIONS

1. Preheat oven to 350°F (175°C). Coat a 9x13 inch baking dish with cooking spray.

2. Cover bottom of baking dish with 1 package crescent rolls. Layer with salami, ham, and pepperoni. Cover meat with a layer of Provolone cheese and Swiss cheese. Spread ½ of the beaten eggs over the cheese. Top with second package of crescent rolls. Brush with remaining beaten eggs, and sprinkle with Parmesan cheese.

3. Bake, uncovered, in the preheated oven for 25 minutes. Cover with foil, and bake for another 10 minutes.

BLT Wraps

Submitted by: **Karen**

Makes: 4 servings

Preparation: 15 minutes

Cooking: 10 minutes

Ready In: 25 minutes

"I love wraps, but am allergic to mayonnaise, so I designed this wrap to be glued together with melted cheese instead. A good variation is to substitute taco meat and grilled onions for the bacon."

INGREDIENTS

1 pound thick sliced bacon, cut into 1 inch pieces

4 (12 inch) flour tortillas

1 cup shredded Cheddar cheese

½ head iceberg lettuce, shredded

1 tomato, diced

DIRECTIONS

1. Place bacon in a large, deep skillet. Cook over medium-high heat until evenly brown. Drain, and set aside.

2. Place 1 tortilla on a microwave-safe plate. Sprinkle tortilla with ¼ cup cheese. Cook in microwave 1 to 2 minutes, or until cheese is melted. Immediately top with ¼ of the bacon, lettuce, and tomato. Fold sides of tortilla over, then roll up. Repeat with remaining ingredients. Cut each wrap in half before serving.

vegetarian

Canned beans, shelf-stable tofu, ready-made curry pastes and dozens of dried spices all make vegetarian cooking more convenient than ever. Keep your kitchen stocked, and your next meatless meal is only moments away. Do you find yourself using the same few combinations of spices and dried herbs time after time? Take another shortcut by making your own seasoning mixtures — such as Indian, Tex-Mex, Cajun, Greek, Italian, Chinese and Middle Eastern — in advance, and you'll be able to give instant, authentic flavor to every dish.

Ginger Veggie Stir-Fry

Submitted by: **Karla**

Makes: 6 servings

Preparation: 25 minutes

Cooking: 15 minutes

Ready In: 40 minutes

"I just whipped this up one day when I felt like a stir-fry but did not have all the ingredients called for in some of the stir-fry recipes on this site. I used certain veggies I had on hand, but any seasonal veggies may be used. It has a mild ginger flavor that can be enhanced according to taste, and is filling yet light on the tummy! Tofu may be added. Serve over a bed of steamed jasmine rice."

INGREDIENTS

1 tablespoon cornstarch

1½ cloves garlic, crushed

2 teaspoons chopped fresh ginger root, divided

¼ cup vegetable oil, divided

1 small head broccoli, cut into florets

½ cup snow peas

¾ cup julienned carrots

½ cup halved green beans

2 tablespoons soy sauce

2½ tablespoons water

¼ cup chopped onion

½ tablespoon salt

DIRECTIONS

1. In a large bowl, blend cornstarch, garlic, 1 teaspoon ginger, and 2 tablespoons vegetable oil until cornstarch is dissolved. Mix in broccoli, snow peas, carrots, and green beans, tossing to lightly coat.

2. Heat remaining 2 tablespoons oil in a large skillet or wok over medium heat. Cook vegetables in oil for 2 minutes, stirring constantly to prevent burning. Stir in soy sauce and water. Mix in onion, salt, and remaining 1 teaspoon ginger. Cook until vegetables are tender but still crisp.

Owen's Veggie Stir-Fry

Submitted by: **Dell**

Makes: 4 servings

Preparation: 20 minutes

Cooking: 15 minutes

Ready In: 35 minutes

"Stir-frying is very quick, and helps retain the flavor of the vegetables. This is a recipe all vegetarians have to try! Fluffy white rice is the perfect complement to this dish."

INGREDIENTS

1 teaspoon cornstarch

2 tablespoons water

1 tablespoon soy sauce

2 tablespoons olive oil

3 tablespoons vegetable oil

1 carrot, sliced

1 red bell pepper, chopped

1 zucchini, sliced

2/3 cup fresh corn kernels

1 clove crushed garlic

4 green onions, sliced

1 1/3 cups bean sprouts

DIRECTIONS

1. Whisk together the cornstarch and water in a small bowl. Mix in the soy sauce and olive oil, and set aside.

2. Heat the vegetable oil in a skillet or wok over medium-high heat. Sauté the carrot, pepper, and zucchini in oil for about 5 minutes. Stir in the corn, garlic, green onions, and bean sprouts. Pour in the soy sauce mixture. Cook and stir for about 5 minutes, or until vegetables are tender but crisp. Serve immediately.

Garbanzo Stir-Fry

Submitted by: **June**

Makes: 4 servings

Preparation: 15 minutes

Cooking: 30 minutes

Ready In: 45 minutes

"This garbanzo bean and veggie stir-fry is great because you can add as many or as few ingredients as you like."

INGREDIENTS

2 tablespoons olive oil

1 tablespoon chopped fresh oregano

1 tablespoon chopped fresh basil

1 clove garlic, crushed

ground black pepper to taste

1 (15 ounce) can garbanzo beans, drained and rinsed

1 large zucchini, halved and sliced

½ cup sliced mushrooms

1 tablespoon chopped fresh cilantro

1 tomato, chopped

DIRECTIONS

1. Heat oil in a large skillet over medium heat. Stir in oregano, basil, garlic, and pepper. Add the garbanzo beans and zucchini, stirring well to coat with oil and herbs. Cook, covered, for 10 minutes, stirring occasionally.

2. Stir in mushrooms and cilantro, and cook until tender, stirring occasionally. Place the chopped tomato on top of the mixture. Cover, and let the tomatoes steam for a few minutes, but don't let them get mushy. Serve immediately.

Chickpea Curry

Submitted by: **Aminah A. Rahman**

Makes: 8 servings

Preparation: 10 minutes

Cooking: 30 minutes

Ready In: 40 minutes

"We usually recommend preparing the beans at home, but using canned chickpeas allows for a fast, convenient dish."

INGREDIENTS

2 tablespoons vegetable oil

2 onions, minced

2 cloves garlic, minced

2 teaspoons fresh ginger root, finely chopped

6 whole cloves

2 (2 inch) sticks cinnamon, crushed

1 teaspoon ground cumin

1 teaspoon ground coriander

1 teaspoon salt

1 teaspoon cayenne pepper

1 teaspoon ground turmeric

2 (15 ounce) cans garbanzo beans

1 cup chopped fresh cilantro

DIRECTIONS

1. Heat oil in a large frying pan over medium heat, and fry onions until tender.

2. Stir in garlic, ginger, cloves, cinnamon, cumin, coriander, salt, cayenne, and turmeric. Cook for 1 minute over medium heat, stirring constantly. Mix in garbanzo beans and their liquid. Continue to cook and stir until all ingredients are well blended and heated through. Remove from heat. Stir in cilantro just before serving, reserving 1 tablespoon for garnish.

Coconut Curry Tofu

Submitted by: **Kathy Collins**

Makes: 6 servings

Preparation: 25 minutes

Cooking: 15 minutes

Ready In: 40 minutes

"My vegetarian daughter-in-law gave me this recipe for a creamy coconut milk, spicy curry, and ginger tofu dish! I serve it over rice."

INGREDIENTS

2 bunches green onions

1 (14 ounce) can light coconut milk

1/4 cup soy sauce, divided

1/2 teaspoon brown sugar

1 1/2 teaspoons curry powder

1 teaspoon minced fresh ginger

2 teaspoons chile paste

1 pound firm tofu, cut into 3/4 inch cubes

4 roma (plum) tomatoes, chopped

1 yellow bell pepper, thinly sliced

4 ounces fresh mushrooms, chopped

1/4 cup chopped fresh basil

4 cups chopped bok choy

salt to taste

DIRECTIONS

1. Remove white parts of green onions, and finely chop. Slice the remaining green parts of the onion into two inch pieces.

2. In a large heavy skillet over medium heat, mix coconut milk, 3 tablespoons soy sauce, brown sugar, curry powder, ginger, and chile paste. Bring to a boil.

3. Stir tofu, tomatoes, yellow pepper, mushrooms, and finely chopped green onions into the skillet. Cover, and cook 5 minutes, stirring occasionally. Mix in basil and bok choy. Season with salt and remaining soy sauce. Continue cooking 5 minutes, or until vegetables are tender but crisp. Garnish with remaining green onion.

Mushroom Risotto

Submitted by: **Sarah**

Makes: 4 servings

Preparation: 10 minutes

Cooking: 35 minutes

Ready In: 45 minutes

"Delicious mushroom risotto made with vegetable broth, cream, and a variety of fresh vegetables. Serve as a side dish or filling main course."

INGREDIENTS

1 tablespoon olive oil

3 small onions, finely chopped

1 clove garlic, crushed

1 teaspoon minced fresh parsley

1 teaspoon minced celery

salt and pepper to taste

1 1/2 cups sliced fresh mushrooms

1 cup whole milk

1/4 cup heavy cream

1 cup rice

5 cups vegetable stock

1 teaspoon butter

1 cup grated Parmesan cheese

DIRECTIONS

1. Heat olive oil in a large skillet over medium-high heat. Sauté the onion and garlic in the olive oil until onion is tender and garlic is lightly browned. Remove garlic, and stir in the parsley, celery, salt, and pepper. Cook until celery is tender, then add the mushrooms. Reduce heat to low, and continue cooking until the mushrooms are soft.

2. Pour the milk and cream into the skillet, and stir in the rice. Heat to a simmer. Add one cup of stock, and stir continuously until completely absorbed. Repeat with remaining stock.

3. When the rice is tender and all liquid is absorbed, stir in the butter and Parmesan cheese, and remove from heat. Serve hot.

Stuffed Peppers My Way

Submitted by: **Sandy**

Makes: 2 servings

Preparation: 20 minutes

Cooking: 40 minutes

Ready In: 1 hour

"Roasted green bell peppers are stuffed with feta cheese and a mixture of rice and green onions."

INGREDIENTS

1 cup water

½ cup uncooked Arborio rice

2 green bell peppers, halved and seeded

1 tablespoon olive oil

2 green onions, thinly sliced

1 teaspoon dried basil

1 teaspoon Italian seasoning

1 teaspoon salt

1 pinch ground black pepper

1 tomato, diced

½ cup crumbled feta cheese

DIRECTIONS

1. Preheat oven to 400°F (200°C). Lightly grease a baking sheet.

2. In a medium saucepan, bring water to a boil. Stir in the rice. Reduce heat, cover, and simmer for 20 minutes. Remove from heat, and set aside.

3. Place the peppers cut-side down on the prepared baking sheet. Roast 25 to 30 minutes in the preheated oven, or until tender and skin starts to brown.

4. While the peppers are roasting, heat oil in a medium skillet over medium-high heat. Cook the onions, basil, Italian seasoning, salt, and pepper in oil for 2 to 3 minutes. Stir in the tomato, and cook for 5 minutes. Spoon in the cooked rice, and stir until heated through. Remove from heat, mix in the feta cheese, and spoon the mixture into the pepper halves.

5. Return to the oven for 5 minutes. Serve immediately.

Quick and Easy Stuffed Peppers

Submitted by: **Jen**

Makes: 4 servings

Preparation: 15 minutes

Cooking: 15 minutes

Ready In: 30 minutes

"This microwave recipe is quick and very simple, and is a good meal for a busy work week. You can use any color peppers you like. Try using garbanzos instead of the kidney beans for a variation on this recipe."

INGREDIENTS

2 large red bell peppers, halved and seeded

1 (8 ounce) can stewed tomatoes, with liquid

1/3 cup quick-cooking brown rice

2 tablespoons hot water

2 green onions, thinly sliced

1/2 cup frozen corn kernels, thawed and drained

1/2 (15 ounce) can kidney beans, drained and rinsed

1/4 teaspoon crushed red pepper flakes

1/2 cup shredded mozzarella cheese

1 tablespoon grated Parmesan cheese

DIRECTIONS

1. Arrange pepper halves in a 9 inch square glass baking dish. Cover dish with plastic wrap. Poke a few holes in the plastic wrap for vents, and heat 4 minutes in the microwave, or until tender.

2. In a medium bowl, mix tomatoes and their liquid, rice, and water. Cover with plastic, and cook in the microwave for 4 minutes, or until rice is cooked.

3. Stir green onions, corn, kidney beans, and red pepper flakes into the tomato mixture. Heat in the microwave for 3 minutes, or until heated through.

4. Spoon hot tomato mixture evenly into pepper halves, and cover with plastic wrap. Poke a few holes in the plastic to vent steam, and heat in the microwave 4 minutes. Remove plastic, sprinkle with mozzarella cheese and Parmesan cheese, and allow to stand 1 to 2 minutes before serving.

Tofu Parmigiana

Submitted by: **Jill B. Mittelstadt**

Makes: 4 servings

Preparation: 25 minutes

Cooking: 20 minutes

Ready In: 45 minutes

"Breaded tofu a la parmigiana. You'll just about swear this is eggplant or veal! One of my husband's favorites, and he doesn't even suspect! Serve with a simple crisp green salad, angel hair pasta and garlic bread."

INGREDIENTS

½ cup seasoned bread crumbs

5 tablespoons grated Parmesan cheese

2 teaspoons dried oregano, divided

salt to taste

ground black pepper to taste

1 (12 ounce) package firm tofu

2 tablespoons olive oil

1 (8 ounce) can tomato sauce

½ teaspoon dried basil

1 clove garlic, minced

4 ounces shredded mozzarella cheese

DIRECTIONS

1. In a small bowl, combine bread crumbs, 2 tablespoons Parmesan cheese, 1 teaspoon oregano, salt, and black pepper.

2. Slice tofu into ¼ inch thick slices, and place in bowl of cold water. One at a time, press tofu slices into crumb mixture, turning to coat all sides.

3. Heat oil in a medium skillet over medium heat. Cook tofu slices until crisp on one side. Drizzle with a bit more olive oil, turn, and brown on the other side.

4. Combine tomato sauce, basil, garlic, and remaining oregano. Place a thin layer of sauce in an 8 inch square baking pan. Arrange tofu slices in the pan. Spoon remaining sauce over tofu. Top with shredded mozzarella and remaining 3 tablespoons Parmesan.

5. Bake at 400°F (205°C) for 20 minutes.

Spaghetti Squash

Submitted by: **James**

Makes: 6 servings

Preparation: 15 minutes

Cooking: 30 minutes

Ready In: 45 minutes

"The flesh of spaghetti squash comes out in long strands, very much resembling the noodles for which it is named. In this recipe, the 'noodles' are tossed with vegetables and feta cheese. You can substitute different vegetables, but be sure to use ones that have contrasting colors."

INGREDIENTS

1 spaghetti squash, halved lengthwise and seeded

2 tablespoons vegetable oil

1 onion, chopped

1 clove garlic, minced

1½ cups chopped tomatoes

¾ cup crumbled feta cheese

3 tablespoons sliced black olives

2 tablespoons chopped fresh basil

DIRECTIONS

1. Preheat oven to 350°F (175°C). Lightly grease a baking sheet.

2. Place spaghetti squash cut sides down on the prepared baking sheet, and bake 30 minutes in the preheated oven, or until a sharp knife can be inserted with only a little resistance. Remove squash from oven, and set aside to cool enough to be easily handled.

3. Meanwhile, heat oil in a skillet over medium heat. Sauté onion in oil until tender. Add garlic, and sauté for 2 to 3 minutes. Stir in the tomatoes, and cook only until tomatoes are warm.

4. Use a large spoon to scoop the stringy pulp from the squash, and place in a medium bowl. Toss with the sautéed vegetables, feta cheese, olives, and basil. Serve warm.

Mexican Bean Pie

Submitted by: **Adele**

Makes: 6 servings

Preparation: 15 minutes

Cooking: 30 minutes

Ready In: 45 minutes

"A quick easy tortilla pie filled with a spicy bean and veggie filling. You can replace the Cheddar cheese with Monterey Jack or any other cheese you like. Top the pie with sour cream and your favorite salsa. Add extra fiber to your diet by using whole wheat tortillas!"

INGREDIENTS

1 (15 ounce) can black beans, drained and rinsed

1 (15 ounce) can pinto beans, drained

1 (16 ounce) can refried beans

1 (2 ounce) can sliced black olives

1/2 (15.25 ounce) can whole kernel corn, drained

1/2 cup chopped green bell pepper

1 jalapeno pepper, seeded and minced

1 tablespoon ground cumin

1 tablespoon chili powder

ground black pepper to taste

5 (10 inch) whole wheat tortillas

1 1/2 cups shredded Cheddar cheese

1/2 cup salsa (optional)

1/2 cup sour cream (optional)

DIRECTIONS

1. Preheat oven to 350°F (175°C). Lightly grease a 10 inch round cake pan or springform pan.

2. In a large saucepan over medium-high heat, mix black beans, pinto beans, refried beans, olives, corn, bell pepper, and jalapeno pepper. Season with cumin, chili power, and black pepper. Cook and stir until thickened, about 10 minutes.

3. Lay one tortilla flat on the bottom of the prepared baking pan. Spread 1/4 of the bean mixture on the tortilla. Sprinkle 1/4 cup Cheddar cheese lightly over the bean mixture. Repeat layering, ending with a tortilla. Top with remaining Cheddar cheese.

4. Bake 20 minutes in the preheated oven. Allow to cool slightly before serving. Serve with salsa and sour cream for garnish.

Veggie Ranch Pizza

Submitted by: **Darlene**

Makes: 10 servings

Preparation: 15 minutes

Cooking: 15 minutes

Ready In: 30 minutes

"Delicious and loaded with fresh veggies, this is pizza for people who want a change from tomato sauce. Use any fresh veggies and any pizza crust. Use light dressing and reduced-fat cheese for an even more healthful meal."

INGREDIENTS

1 unbaked pizza crust

1 1/2 cups Ranch-style salad dressing

2 cups shredded Cheddar cheese

1/2 cup shredded carrots

1/2 cup chopped cauliflower

1/2 cup chopped fresh broccoli

1/2 cup chopped onion

1/2 cup chopped red bell pepper

1/2 cup sliced fresh mushrooms

1 pound mozzarella cheese, shredded

DIRECTIONS

1. Preheat oven to 350°F (175°C).

2. Place pizza crust on a pizza pan or baking sheet, and spread dressing evenly over the top. Sprinkle with Cheddar cheese, followed by carrots, cauliflower, broccoli, onion, red pepper, and mushrooms. Top with mozzarella cheese.

3. Bake in preheated oven for 15 to 20 minutes, until vegetables are tender, and cheese is melted and lightly browned.

Eggplant and Pepper Parmesan Sandwiches

Submitted by: **Marlena**

Makes: 4 sandwiches

Preparation: 15 minutes

Cooking: 10 minutes

Ready In: 25 minutes

"Smoky grilled veggies, rich tapenade, and tangy goat cheese make these sandwiches hearty and satisfying. A friend of mine made these and I loved them. By the next week, I was craving one of these delicious sandwiches."

INGREDIENTS

1 eggplant, seeded and cut lengthwise into 1/4 inch slices

1 red bell pepper, sliced into thin strips

salt and pepper to taste

1 French baguette

2 ounces soft goat cheese

1/4 cup tapenade (olive spread)

1/4 cup grated Parmesan cheese

DIRECTIONS

1. Preheat the oven broiler.

2. Place the eggplant and red bell pepper on a medium baking sheet, and season with salt and pepper. Broil 5 to 10 minutes, until tender and slightly browned.

3. Cut baguette in half lengthwise. Spread bottom half with goat cheese, followed by tapenade. Layer with eggplant and red pepper, then sprinkle with Parmesan cheese. Cover with top half of baguette. Cut into 4 pieces. Serve hot or cold.

Butter Bean Burgers

Submitted by: **Silverwolf**

Makes: 4 servings

Preparation: 15 minutes

Cooking: 10 minutes

Ready In: 25 minutes

"This is served in place of meat for a main meal, or great as a sandwich with your favorite toppings."

INGREDIENTS

1 (15 ounce) can butter beans, drained

1 small onion, chopped

1 tablespoon finely chopped jalapeno pepper

6 saltine crackers, crushed

1 egg, beaten

½ cup shredded Cheddar cheese

¼ teaspoon garlic powder

salt and pepper to taste

¼ cup vegetable oil

DIRECTIONS

1. In a medium bowl, mash butter beans. Mix in onion, jalapeno pepper, crushed crackers, egg, cheese, garlic powder, salt, and pepper. Divide into 4 equal parts, and shape into patties.

2. Heat oil in a large skillet over medium-high heat; use more or less oil to reach ¼ inch in depth. Fry patties until golden, about 5 minutes on each side.

Awesome Grilled Cheese Sandwiches

Submitted by: **Michelle**

Makes: 9 servings

Preparation: 10 minutes

Cooking: 15 minutes

Ready In: 25 minutes

"My husband and I were sick of frying grilled cheeses on the stove because you have so many pieces of bread to use, and you have to stand there for a long time if you feed up to six people like we do. So we came up with this idea."

INGREDIENTS

18 slices bread

4 tablespoons butter

9 slices Cheddar cheese

DIRECTIONS

1. Preheat oven to 450°F (230°C).

2. Butter one side of 9 slices of bread, and place butter-side down on a baking sheet. Arrange cheese on each slice of bread. Spread butter on 9 remaining slices of bread, and place them buttered-side up on top of the cheese.

3. Bake in preheated oven for 6 to 8 minutes. Flip the sandwiches, and bake an additional 6 to 8 minutes, or until golden brown.

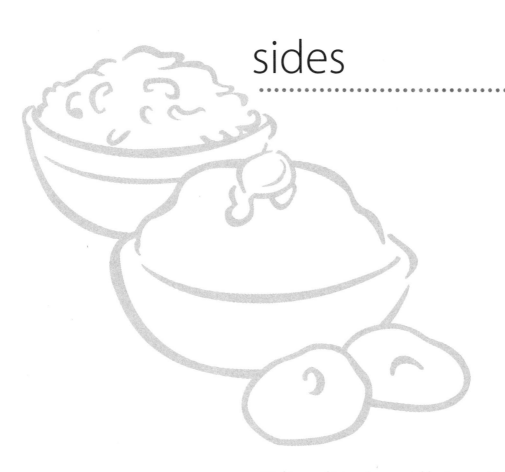

sides

Washing and trimming vegetables is a great job for young cooks, so if there are kids in your house, throw aprons on them and put them to work! With green beans and asparagus, they can trim off the ends and snap them in half without ever touching a knife. Likewise, lettuce, spinach and herbs can all be torn easily by little hands. Soft things like mushrooms and zucchini can be safely sliced with small, dull knives. Carrots, potatoes, zucchini and cheese are also easily handled with kid-safe prep tools, like graters and peelers.

Oven Roasted Potatoes

Submitted by: **Janet**

Makes: 4 servings

Preparation: 15 minutes

Cooking: 30 minutes

Ready In: 45 minutes

"A great roasted potato side dish made with olive oil and herbs."

INGREDIENTS

⅛ cup olive oil

1 tablespoon minced garlic

½ teaspoon dried basil

½ teaspoon dried marjoram

½ teaspoon dried dill weed

½ teaspoon dried thyme

½ teaspoon dried oregano

½ teaspoon dried parsley

½ teaspoon crushed red pepper flakes

½ teaspoon salt

4 large potatoes, peeled and cubed

DIRECTIONS

1. Preheat oven to 475°F (245°C).

2. In a large bowl, combine oil, garlic, basil, marjoram, dill weed, thyme, oregano, parsley, red pepper flakes, and salt. Stir in potatoes until evenly coated. Place potatoes in a single layer on a roasting pan or baking sheet.

3. Roast for 20 to 30 minutes in the preheated oven, turning occasionally to brown on all sides.

Bella's Rosemary Red Potatoes

Submitted by: **Bellarouge**

Makes: 4 servings

Preparation: 10 minutes

Cooking: 30 minutes

Ready In: 40 minutes

"The simplest, most elegant side dish ever! This is the best way to impress company without any extra effort. Substitute 1 teaspoon dried rosemary if you do not have fresh rosemary. Bon appetit!"

INGREDIENTS

6 red potatoes, scrubbed and cut into wedges

3 tablespoons butter, melted

3 tablespoons vegetable oil

1 tablespoon chopped fresh rosemary

salt and pepper to taste

DIRECTIONS

1. Preheat oven to 375°F (190°C).

2. Mix together melted butter and oil, then pour into a 9x13 inch baking dish. Place the potatoes into the dish, and stir until coated. Sprinkle with rosemary, salt, and pepper. Cover with aluminum foil.

3. Bake in the preheated oven for 30 minutes, or until the potatoes are tender. Stir the potatoes occasionally to ensure even cooking.

Cheesy Ranch New Red Potatoes

Submitted by: **F.R.**

Makes: 4 servings

Preparation: 5 minutes

Cooking: 30 minutes

Ready In: 35 minutes

"My family requests these potatoes all the time. They are awesome and so easy!"

INGREDIENTS

12 small new red potatoes, scrubbed and halved

1 cup Ranch-style salad dressing

1 (8 ounce) package shredded Colby-Monterey Jack cheese

1 teaspoon freshly ground black pepper

DIRECTIONS

1. Preheat oven to 350°F (175°C).

2. Place potatoes in a large saucepan over medium heat, and cover with water. Bring to a boil, and cook 10 minutes, or until tender; drain.

3. Place cooked potatoes on an ungreased cookie sheet with the cut side up. Spread a spoonful of dressing on the top of each potato half. Sprinkle with cheese, and lightly dust with pepper.

4. Bake in the preheated oven for 5 minutes, or until cheese is melted.

Suzy's Mashed Red Potatoes

Submitted by: **B.T.**

Makes: 8 servings

Preparation: 10 minutes

Cooking: 20 minutes

Ready In: 30 minutes

"These are the best I've had! Red potato skins are full of flavor!"

INGREDIENTS

2 pounds small red potatoes, quartered

1/2 cup butter

1/2 cup milk

1/4 cup sour cream

salt and pepper to taste

DIRECTIONS

1. Bring a large pot of lightly salted water to a boil. Add potatoes, and cook until tender but still firm, about 10 minutes. Drain, and place in a large bowl.

2. Combine potatoes with butter, milk, sour cream, salt, and pepper. Mash together until smooth and creamy.

Cowboy Mashed Potatoes

Submitted by: **Bruticus**

Makes: 10 servings

Preparation: 20 minutes

Cooking: 20 minutes

Ready In: 40 minutes

"Quick, easy and delicious mashed potatoes with corn and carrots."

INGREDIENTS

1 pound red potatoes

1 pound Yukon Gold (yellow) potatoes

1 fresh jalapeno pepper, sliced

12 ounces baby carrots

4 cloves garlic

1 (10 ounce) package frozen white corn, thawed

1/4 cup butter

1/2 cup shredded Cheddar cheese

salt and pepper to taste

DIRECTIONS

1. Place red potatoes, yellow potatoes, jalapeno pepper, carrots and garlic cloves in a large pot. Cover with water, and bring to a boil over high heat. Cook 15 to 20 minutes, or until potatoes are tender. Drain water from pot.

2. Stir in corn and butter. Mash the mixture with a potato masher until butter is melted and potatoes have reached desired consistency. Mix in cheese, salt, and pepper. Serve hot.

Garlic Mashed Potatoes

Submitted by: **Lorna**

Makes: 4 servings

Preparation: 10 minutes

Cooking: 25 minutes

Ready In: 35 minutes

"These garlic mashed potatoes are rich and very tasty! For a creamier texture, use heavy cream in place of the milk. These are also terrific topped with green onions."

INGREDIENTS

8 potatoes, peeled and quartered

1/2 cup milk

1/4 cup butter

2 cloves garlic, minced

salt to taste

1 pinch ground white pepper

2 tablespoons sesame seeds

DIRECTIONS

1. Bring a large pot of water to boil; add potatoes, and boil until soft, about 20 to 25 minutes. Drain, and place in a large bowl.

2. Combine potatoes with milk, butter, garlic, salt, and pepper. Mix with an electric mixer or potato masher to your desired consistency. Sprinkle with sesame seeds.

Emily's Famous Fried Potatoes

Submitted by: **Emily B.**

Makes: 6 servings

Preparation: 20 minutes

Cooking: 20 minutes

Ready In: 40 minutes

"This is a very tasty potato recipe that is also great for using up leftover baked potatoes. The vinegar gives the spinach a sweet flavor. I like to crumble feta cheese over them too!"

INGREDIENTS

6 medium red potatoes, diced

2 tablespoons light olive oil

1/2 red onion

4 cloves garlic

1 tablespoon chopped fresh basil

1 teaspoon chopped fresh rosemary

1 teaspoon chopped fresh oregano

1 bunch fresh spinach, rinsed and stems removed

2 tablespoons red wine vinegar

salt and ground black pepper to taste

DIRECTIONS

1. Place potatoes in a large saucepan over medium heat, and cover with water. Bring to a boil, and cook until tender. Drain, and set aside.

2. Heat oil in a large, heavy skillet over medium heat. Sauté the onion and garlic with the basil, rosemary, and oregano until the onion is just tender. Throw in the potatoes, and fry until lightly browned. Cover with spinach, and sprinkle with vinegar. Cover, and cook on low until the spinach is tender.

3. Remove from heat, and stir the mixture together. Season with salt and pepper.

Zucchini Patties

Submitted by: **Sherlie A. Magaret**

Makes: 12 patties

Preparation: 10 minutes

Cooking: 20 minutes

Ready In: 30 minutes

"These cheesy zucchini patties are an excellent way to use up that abundance of zucchini from the garden. Serve with a bit of tomato sauce or sour cream dabbed on top."

INGREDIENTS

2 cups grated zucchini

2 eggs, beaten

1/4 cup chopped onion

1/2 cup all-purpose flour

1/2 cup grated Parmesan cheese

1/2 cup shredded mozzarella cheese

salt to taste

2 tablespoons vegetable oil

DIRECTIONS

1. In a medium bowl, combine the zucchini, eggs, onion, flour, Parmesan cheese, mozzarella cheese, and salt. Stir well enough to distribute ingredients evenly.

2. Heat a small amount of oil in a skillet over medium-high heat. Drop zucchini mixture by heaping tablespoonfuls, and cook for a few minutes on each side until golden.

Corn and Zucchini Melody

Submitted by: **Gail**

Makes: 5 servings

Preparation: 5 minutes

Cooking: 25 minutes

Ready In: 30 minutes

"Zucchini, corn, and onions combined with chopped bacon and cheese. A quick and easy way to use some fresh veggies from your garden!"

INGREDIENTS

4 slices bacon

2 cups chopped zucchini

1½ cups fresh corn kernels

1 small onion, chopped

1 pinch pepper

¼ cup shredded Monterey Jack cheese

DIRECTIONS

1. Place bacon in a large, deep skillet. Cook over medium-high heat until evenly brown. Reserve 1 tablespoon of drippings. Drain bacon, chop, and set aside.

2. Heat the bacon drippings in the skillet over medium heat. Sauté the zucchini, corn, and onion until tender but still crisp, about 10 minutes. Season with pepper. Spoon vegetables into a bowl, and sprinkle with chopped bacon and shredded cheese.

Fresh Corn and Tomato Casserole

Submitted by: **Ronda Miller**

Makes: 6 servings

Preparation: 15 minutes

Cooking: 45 minutes

Ready In: 1 hour

"This casserole is wonderful for a backyard picnic. It uses all fresh ingredients and simply contains corn, tomatoes and bacon. A great complement for a barbecue."

INGREDIENTS

4 slices bacon

8 ears fresh corn

¼ cup butter

1 teaspoon salt

2 large tomatoes, sliced

DIRECTIONS

1. Preheat oven to 350°F (175°C). Place bacon in a large, deep skillet. Cook over medium-high heat until crisp and evenly brown; drain. Chop bacon, and set aside.

2. Cut corn from cobs. There should be about 4 or 5 cups of corn kernels. Melt butter in a large skillet over medium heat. Add the corn, and cook for about 5 minutes, stirring constantly. Stir in the bacon and salt, and remove from heat.

3. Spread a layer of the corn mixture into the bottom of a 2-quart casserole dish, then layer with tomatoes. Repeat layers twice, ending with tomatoes on the top.

4. Bake uncovered in preheated oven for 30 minutes, or until corn is tender.

Daddy's Fried Corn and Onions

Submitted by: **Michelle Lewis**

Makes: 4 servings

Preparation: 10 minutes

Cooking: 15 minutes

Ready In: 25 minutes

"Combining my two favorites, fried onions and fresh corn, my husband came up with this very simple, delicious side dish."

INGREDIENTS

4 ears fresh corn

2 tablespoons butter

1 small sweet onion, diced

salt and pepper to taste

DIRECTIONS

1. Cut corn kernels from cob. Melt butter in a medium skillet over medium heat. Sauté corn kernels just until tender, then mix in onion. Continue to sauté until onion is just beginning to turn crispy. Season with salt and pepper. Enjoy warm or cold.

Orange Glazed Carrots

Submitted by: **Heidi**

Makes: 4 servings

Preparation: 5 minutes

Cooking: 15 minutes

Ready In: 20 minutes

"A wonderfully easy glazed carrot recipe that the whole family will enjoy. Great for special occasions or an every day meal."

INGREDIENTS

1 pound baby carrots

¼ cup orange juice

3 tablespoons brown sugar

2 tablespoons butter

1 pinch salt

DIRECTIONS

1. Place carrots in a shallow saucepan, and cover with water. Boil until tender. Drain, and return carrots to pan.

2. Pour orange juice over carrots, and mix well. Simmer over medium heat for about 5 minutes. Stir in brown sugar, butter, and salt. Heat until butter and sugar melt.

Buttery Cooked Carrots

Submitted by: **Rebecca**

"Sweet cooked carrots that even my carrot-hating family loves. There are never leftovers."

INGREDIENTS

1 pound baby carrots

¼ cup margarine

⅓ cup brown sugar

DIRECTIONS

1. Cook carrots in a large pot of boiling water until tender. Drain off most of the liquid, leaving bottom of pan covered with water. Set the carrots aside.

2. Stir margarine and brown sugar into the water. Simmer and stir until the margarine melts. Return carrots to the pot, and toss to coat. Cover, and let sit for a few minutes to allow flavors to mingle.

Cream Peas

Submitted by: **Stephanie Moon**

Makes: 4 servings

Preparation: 5 minutes

Cooking: 10 minutes

Ready In: 15 minutes

"In my search for a good cream pea recipe, I found many, but none that quite matched what I wanted. So I took to my own creativity and came up with this absolutely fabulous recipe. We love it so much we have this on the side quite often."

INGREDIENTS

2 cups frozen green peas, thawed

2/3 cup water

1/8 teaspoon salt

3 tablespoons butter

1/3 cup heavy cream

2 tablespoons all-purpose flour

1 tablespoon white sugar

DIRECTIONS

1. In a medium saucepan, combine peas, water, and salt. Bring to a boil, then stir in butter.

2. In a small bowl, whisk together cream, flour, and sugar. Stir mixture into peas. Cook over medium-high heat until thick and bubbly, about 5 minutes.

Green Bean and Mushroom Medley

Submitted by: **Michele**

Makes: 6 servings

Preparation: 20 minutes

Cooking: 15 minutes

Ready In: 35 minutes

"This is a great vegetable side dish. This is always served at our family gatherings with no leftovers."

INGREDIENTS

½ pound fresh green beans, cut into 1-inch lengths

2 carrots, cut into thick strips

¼ cup butter

1 onion, sliced

½ pound fresh mushrooms, sliced

1 teaspoon salt

½ teaspoon seasoned salt

¼ teaspoon garlic salt

¼ teaspoon white pepper

DIRECTIONS

1. Place green beans and carrots in 1 inch of boiling water. Cover, and cook until tender but still firm. Drain.

2. Melt butter in a large skillet over medium heat. Sauté onions and mushrooms until almost tender. Reduce heat, cover, and simmer 3 minutes. Stir in green beans, carrots, salt, seasoned salt, garlic salt, and white pepper. Cover, and cook for 5 minutes over medium heat.

Garlic Green Beans

Submitted by: **Ericka Ettinger**

Makes: 5 servings

Preparation: 10 minutes

Cooking: 15 minutes

Ready In: 25 minutes

"Caramelized garlic and cheese! Is there anything better with green beans? You'd better make plenty for everyone!"

INGREDIENTS

1 tablespoon butter

3 tablespoons olive oil

1 medium head garlic - peeled and sliced

2 (14.5 ounce) cans green beans, drained

salt and pepper to taste

¼ cup grated Parmesan cheese

DIRECTIONS

1. In a large skillet over medium heat, melt butter with olive oil; add garlic, and cook until lightly browned, stirring frequently. Stir in green beans, and season with salt and pepper. Cook until beans are tender, about 10 minutes. Remove from heat, and sprinkle with Parmesan cheese.

Lemon Green Beans with Walnuts

Submitted by: **Karen David**

Makes: 6 servings

Preparation: 15 minutes

Cooking: 15 minutes

Ready In: 30 minutes

"Steamed green beans tossed with butter, lemon zest, lemon juice and toasted walnuts. This is excellent with asparagus also. Pecans can be substituted for walnuts."

INGREDIENTS

½ cup chopped walnuts

1 pound green beans, trimmed and cut into 2 inch pieces

2½ tablespoons unsalted butter, melted

1 lemon, juiced and zested

salt and pepper to taste

DIRECTIONS

1. Preheat oven to 375°F (190°C). Arrange nuts in a single layer on a baking sheet. Toast in the preheated oven until lightly browned, approximately 5 to 10 minutes.

2. Place green beans in a steamer over 1 inch of boiling water, and cover. Steam for 8 to 10 minutes, or until tender, but still bright green.

3. Place cooked beans in a large bowl, and toss with butter, lemon juice, and lemon zest. Season with salt and pepper. Transfer beans to a serving dish, and sprinkle with toasted walnuts. Serve immediately.

Lemon Pepper Green Beans

Submitted by: **Annette Byrdy**

Makes: 6 servings

Preparation: 5 minutes

Cooking: 20 minutes

Ready In: 25 minutes

"These green beans are easy and delicious. They are a bit tangy, spicy, and crunchy with the almonds. My family's favorite!"

INGREDIENTS

1 pound fresh green beans, rinsed and trimmed

2 tablespoons butter

¼ cup sliced almonds

2 teaspoons lemon pepper

DIRECTIONS

1. Place green beans in a steamer over 1 inch of boiling water. Cover, and cook until tender but still firm, about 10 minutes; drain.

2. Meanwhile, melt butter in a skillet over medium heat. Sauté almonds until lightly browned. Season with lemon pepper. Stir in green beans, and toss to coat.

Asparagus with Parmesan Crust

Submitted by: **Kimber**

Makes: 6 servings

Preparation: 10 minutes

Cooking: 15 minutes

Ready In: 25 minutes

"Can be used as either a side dish or a warm appetizer. Indulge yourself with the finest balsamic vinegar you can find, and enjoy!"

INGREDIENTS

1 pound thin asparagus spears

1 tablespoon extra virgin olive oil

1 ounce shaved Parmesan cheese

freshly ground black pepper to taste

¼ cup balsamic vinegar, or to taste

DIRECTIONS

1. Preheat oven to 450°F (230°C).

2. Place asparagus on a baking sheet. Drizzle with olive oil, and toss to coat. Arrange asparagus spears in a single layer. Spread Parmesan cheese over asparagus, and season with freshly ground black pepper.

3. Bake 12 to 15 minutes in the preheated oven, until cheese is melted and asparagus is tender but crisp. Serve immediately on warm plates, sprinkling with balsamic vinegar to taste.

Pan-Fried Asparagus

Submitted by: **Kim**

Makes: 4 servings

Preparation: 5 minutes

Cooking: 15 minutes

Ready In: 25 minutes

"This garlic asparagus dish is a Northern Italian side dish. My family loves it! Even the kids!"

INGREDIENTS

¼ cup butter

2 tablespoons olive oil

1 teaspoon coarse salt

¼ teaspoon ground black pepper

3 cloves garlic, minced

½ pound fresh asparagus spears, trimmed

DIRECTIONS

1. Melt butter in a skillet over medium-high heat. Stir in the olive oil, salt, and pepper. Cook garlic in butter for a minute, but do not brown. Add asparagus, and cook for 10 minutes, turning asparagus to ensure even cooking.

Pat's Mushroom Sauté

Submitted by: **Lanni**

Makes: 4 servings

Preparation: 5 minutes

Cooking: 30 minutes

Ready In: 35 minutes

"My son-in-law makes the best sautéed mushrooms; and now, so do I! Eat them hot out of the pan; they don't reheat well."

INGREDIENTS

2 tablespoons butter

1/2 tablespoon olive oil

1/2 tablespoon balsamic vinegar

1 clove garlic, minced

1/8 teaspoon dried oregano

1 pound button mushrooms, sliced

DIRECTIONS

1. Melt butter with oil in a large skillet over medium heat. Stir in balsamic vinegar, garlic, oregano, and mushrooms. Sauté for 20 to 30 minutes, or until tender.

Fried Cabbage II

Submitted by: **Jen**

Makes: 6 servings

Preparation: 20 minutes

Cooking: 25 minutes

Ready In: 45 minutes

"Cabbage and onions are sautéed in bacon grease, and served with a splash of vinegar, for a tangy, hearty dish that will surprise you."

INGREDIENTS

3 slices bacon, chopped

¼ cup chopped onion

6 cups cabbage, cut into thin wedges

2 tablespoons water

1 pinch white sugar

salt and pepper to taste

1 tablespoon cider vinegar

DIRECTIONS

1. Place bacon in a large, deep skillet. Cook over medium-high heat until evenly brown. Remove bacon, and set aside.

2. Cook onion in the hot bacon grease until tender. Add cabbage, and stir in water, sugar, salt, and pepper. Cook until cabbage wilts, about 15 minutes. Stir in bacon. Splash with vinegar before serving.

Fried Onion Rings

Submitted by: **Jill**

Makes: 12 servings

Preparation: 15 minutes

Cooking: 20 minutes

Ready In: 45 minutes

"These are very delicate and the best I have had. My ex was a fanatic when it came to onion rings, and thought this recipe to be the best he ever had. Have also made other veggies in this batter. Can be refrigerated or frozen, then reheated in oven or microwave. Carbonated water can be substituted for beer in this recipe."

INGREDIENTS

1 quart vegetable oil for frying

1 cup all-purpose flour

1 cup beer

1 pinch salt

1 pinch ground black pepper

4 onions, peeled and sliced into rings

DIRECTIONS

1. In a large, deep skillet, heat oil to 365°F (180°C).

2. In a medium bowl, combine flour, beer, salt, and pepper. Mix until smooth. Dredge onion slices in the batter, until evenly coated. Deep fry in the hot oil until golden brown. Drain on paper towels.

Fried Okra

Submitted by: **Linda Martin**

Makes: 4 servings
Preparation: 15 minutes
Cooking: 15 minutes
Ready In: 30 minutes

"A simple Southern classic! Okra is dredged in seasoned cornmeal, then fried until golden."

INGREDIENTS

10 pods okra, sliced in 1/4 inch pieces

1 egg, beaten

1 cup cornmeal

1/4 teaspoon salt

1/4 teaspoon ground black pepper

1/2 cup vegetable oil

DIRECTIONS

1. In a small bowl, soak okra in egg for 5 to 10 minutes. In a medium bowl, combine cornmeal, salt, and pepper.

2. Heat oil in a large skillet over medium-high heat. Dredge okra in the cornmeal mixture, coating evenly. Carefully place okra in hot oil; stir continuously. Reduce heat to medium when okra first starts to brown, and cook until golden. Drain on paper towels.

Spanish Rice II

Submitted by: **Dave**

Makes: 4 servings

Preparation: 10 minutes

Cooking: 30 minutes

Ready In: 40 minutes

"Rice is sautéed with onion and green bell pepper, and then simmered with water, chopped tomatoes and spices."

INGREDIENTS

2 tablespoons vegetable oil

1 cup uncooked white rice

1 onion, chopped

½ green bell pepper, chopped

2 cups water

1 (10 ounce) can diced tomatoes and green chiles

2 teaspoons chili powder, or to taste

1 teaspoon salt

DIRECTIONS

1. Heat oil in a deep skillet over medium heat. Sauté rice, onion, and bell pepper until rice is browned and onions are tender.

2. Stir in water and tomatoes. Season with chili powder and salt. Cover, and simmer for 30 minutes, or until rice is cooked and liquid is absorbed.

Very Easy Risotto

Submitted by: **Kim Sanchez**

Makes: 6 servings

Preparation: 10 minutes

Cooking: 30 minutes

Ready In: 40 minutes

"This green onion and Parmesan cheese rice dish is easy, fast and doesn't require constant stirring!"

INGREDIENTS

2 tablespoons butter

²/₃ cup sliced green onion

1¹/₃ cups uncooked long-grain rice

4 cups water

1 teaspoon chicken bouillon granules

¹/₄ teaspoon ground black pepper

³/₄ cup grated Parmesan cheese

DIRECTIONS

1. Melt butter in a large skillet over medium-high heat. Cook green onions in butter briefly, then add the rice. Cook and stir for a few minutes to toast rice. Stir in water, and season with chicken bouillon and pepper. Bring to a boil, then reduce heat to medium-low. Cover, and simmer for 20 minutes.

2. Remove from heat, cover, and let stand for 5 minutes. Stir in the Parmesan cheese.

Couscous with Dried Cherries

Submitted by: **Stephanie Moon**

Makes: 4 servings

Preparation: 5 minutes

Cooking: 10 minutes

Ready In: 20 minutes

"My family loves couscous and this fruity variation is one of our favorites. This is also delicious with other dried fruit such as cranberries and apricots."

INGREDIENTS

1 cup chicken broth

¼ cup water

¼ cup dried sour cherries

1 tablespoon butter

1 pinch salt

ground black pepper to taste

1 cup uncooked couscous

DIRECTIONS

1. In a 2 quart saucepan, combine chicken broth, water, dried cherries, butter, salt, and pepper. Cook over high heat until boiling.

2. Stir in couscous, cover, and remove from heat. Let stand 5 minutes. Fluff with a fork, and serve immediately.

Vicki's Hush Puppies

Submitted by: **Vicki Conley**

Makes: 24 hush puppies
Preparation: 10 minutes
Cooking: 30 minutes
Ready In: 40 minutes

"Hush puppies are a good side for seafood."

INGREDIENTS

2 eggs, beaten

1/2 cup white sugar

1 large onion, diced

1 cup self-rising flour

1 cup self-rising cornmeal

1 quart oil for frying

DIRECTIONS

1. In a medium bowl, mix together eggs, sugar, and onion. Blend in flour and cornmeal.

2. In a deep skillet, heat 2 inches of oil to 365°F (185°C). Drop batter by rounded teaspoonfuls in hot oil, and fry until golden brown. Cook in small batches to maintain oil temperature. Drain briefly on paper towels. Serve hot.

Zucchini Tomato Pie

Submitted by: **Lynn**

Makes: 6 servings

Preparation: 15 minutes

Cooking: 30 minutes

Ready In: 45 minutes

"Zucchini, tomato and onion combined with Parmesan cheese and baked with milk and biscuit mix."

INGREDIENTS

2 cups chopped zucchini

1 cup chopped tomato

1/2 cup chopped onion

1/3 cup grated Parmesan cheese

3/4 cup biscuit baking mix

1/2 cup milk

3 eggs

1/2 teaspoon salt

1/4 teaspoon ground black pepper

DIRECTIONS

1. Preheat oven to 400°F (200°C). Grease a 10 inch pie pan.

2. Combine zucchini, tomato, onion, and Parmesan cheese in prepared pie pan. In a small bowl, combine biscuit mix, milk, eggs, and salt and pepper. Beat until smooth, then pour over vegetable mixture.

3. Bake in preheated oven for 30 minutes, or until a knife inserted into the center comes out clean.

Creamy Broccoli Casserole

Submitted by: **Menda**

Makes: 8 servings

Preparation: 5 minutes

Cooking: 40 minutes

Ready In: 45 minutes

"Wonderful side dish with broccoli and cream cheese. Even my kids like this dish."

INGREDIENTS

1 (16 ounce) package frozen broccoli, thawed

2 tablespoons butter

1/4 teaspoon salt

2 tablespoons all-purpose flour

2 cups milk

1 (8 ounce) package cream cheese, cubed

1 cup crushed buttery round crackers

DIRECTIONS

1. Preheat oven to 350°F (175°C).

2. Place broccoli in a steamer over 1 inch of boiling water, and cover. Cook until tender but still firm, about 4 to 6 minutes; drain.

3. Melt butter in a large saucepan over medium heat. Stir in salt and flour, and then whisk in milk. Cook, stirring constantly, until thick and bubbly. Stir in cream cheese until melted. Remove from heat, and stir in broccoli.

4. Sprinkle ½ cup of crushed crackers over the bottom of a 1 ½ quart casserole dish. Slowly pour the broccoli mixture into the dish, and top with remaining crushed crackers.

5. Bake in preheated oven for 30 minutes.

Yellow Squash Casserole

Submitted by: **Rosalie Carter**

Makes: 8 servings

Preparation: 20 minutes

Cooking: 30 minutes

Ready In: 50 minutes

"Tender squash, gooey cheese and crunchy crackers make this a memorable side dish or a hearty main course. This is a great dish that can be made with low-fat ingredients and is still just as good!"

INGREDIENTS

4 cups sliced yellow squash

1/2 cup chopped onion

35 buttery round crackers, crushed

1 cup shredded Cheddar cheese

2 eggs, beaten

3/4 cup milk

1/4 cup butter, melted

1 teaspoon salt

ground black pepper to taste

2 tablespoons butter

DIRECTIONS

1. Preheat oven to 400°F (200°C).

2. Place squash and onion in a large skillet over medium heat. Pour in a small amount of water. Cover, and cook until squash is tender, about 5 minutes. Drain well, and place in a large bowl.

3. In a medium bowl, mix together cracker crumbs and cheese. Stir half of the cracker mixture into the cooked squash and onions. In a small bowl, mix together eggs and milk, then add to squash mixture. Stir in 1/4 cup melted butter, and season with salt and pepper. Spread into a 9x13 inch baking dish. Sprinkle with remaining cracker mixture, and dot with 2 tablespoons butter.

4. Bake in preheated oven for 25 minutes, or until lightly browned.

Veggie Casserole

Submitted by: **Rachel Query**

Makes: 6 servings

Preparation: 10 minutes

Cooking: 25 minutes

Ready In: 35 minutes

"Green beans, bell pepper and corn are the veggies in this creamy cheese-topped side dish. A great casserole for the busy mom and family, this casserole takes a small amount of time to assemble and bakes in the oven in less than 30 minutes."

INGREDIENTS

1 (14.5 ounce) can French-style green beans, drained

1 (11 ounce) can white corn, drained

1 small onion, chopped

1/2 green bell pepper, chopped

1 (8 ounce) container sour cream

1 (10.75 ounce) can condensed cream of celery soup

1/2 cup shredded sharp Cheddar cheese

salt and pepper to taste

1/2 (16 ounce) package cheese flavored crackers, crushed

1/4 cup butter, melted

DIRECTIONS

1. Preheat oven to 350°F (175°C).

2. In a large bowl, combine green beans, corn, onion, and green bell pepper. Stir in sour cream, condensed soup, and shredded cheese. Season with salt and pepper. Mix well, and spread into a 2 quart casserole dish. In a separate bowl, mix together the crushed crackers and melted butter. Sprinkle over vegetable mixture.

3. Bake in preheated oven, for 25 minutes, or until the top is golden brown.

Zucchini Casserole II

Submitted by: **Bea**

Makes: 8 servings

Preparation: 15 minutes

Cooking: 25 minutes

Ready In: 40 minutes

"This is a tasty way to use up some of your bumper crop of zucchini."

INGREDIENTS

6 cups diced zucchini

1 (10.75 ounce) can condensed cream of mushroom soup

1 cup sour cream

1/2 cup chopped onion

1 cup shredded carrots

1 (6 ounce) package dry bread stuffing mix

1/2 cup butter, melted

DIRECTIONS

1. Preheat oven to 350°F (175°C). Grease a 2 quart casserole dish.

2. In a large saucepan over medium-high heat, cook zucchini in lightly salted water until crisp-tender, about 5 minutes. Drain, and place in a large bowl. Stir in the condensed soup, sour cream, onion, and carrots.

3. In a small bowl, mix together stuffing and melted butter. Spread half of the stuffing mixture in the bottom of the casserole dish, add a layer of the zucchini mixture, and top with remaining stuffing mixture.

4. Bake for 20 minutes in the preheated oven, or until the top is golden brown.

Super Squash

Submitted by: **NDNorton**

Makes: 12 servings

Preparation: 20 minutes

Cooking: 25 minutes

Ready In: 45 minutes

"This is my mom's recipe. This squash casserole is filled with flavor and baked with a wonderful stuffing crust. If you like yellow summer squash, then you'll love this great recipe!"

INGREDIENTS

2 tablespoons butter

3 pounds yellow squash, chopped

2 onions, chopped

1 cup shredded sharp Cheddar cheese

1 cup mayonnaise

3 eggs, beaten

12 saltine crackers, crushed

1 (1 ounce) package dry Ranch-style dressing mix

1 teaspoon salt

2 cups dry bread stuffing mix

½ cup melted butter

DIRECTIONS

1. Preheat oven to 350°F (175°C).

2. Melt 2 tablespoons butter in a large saucepan over medium-high heat. Cook squash and onions until tender. Remove from heat, and stir in Cheddar cheese, mayonnaise, eggs, and crackers. Season with Ranch dressing mix and salt.

3. Spread the squash mixture into a medium baking dish. Mix together stuffing and ½ cup melted butter, and sprinkle over the squash mixture.

4. Bake 20 to 30 minutes in the preheated oven, or until firm and lightly browned.

recipe contributors

index by time; less than 20 minutes

salads

soups

seafood

chicken and turkey

beef and pork

sides

index by time; 20 to 30 minutes

index by time; 30 to 40 minutes

salads

soups

pasta

seafood

chicken and turkey

beef and pork

vegetarian

sides

index

the allrecipes tried & true series

Our *Tried & True* cookbooks feature the very best recipes from the world's greatest home cooks! Allrecipes.com, the #1 recipe website, brings you the "Best of the Best" dishes and treats, selected from over 20,000 recipes! We hand-picked only those recipes that have been awarded 5-star ratings time and time again by our worldwide community of home cooks to fill these books, so you know every dish is a winner.

Current titles include:

Allrecipes Tried & True Favorites; Top 300 Recipes

Treat yourself to America's Favorite Recipes! Filled with the best-loved recipes from Allrecipes.com - these have all won repeated standing ovations from millions of home cooks and their families, intrepid eaters and picky kids alike. *Tried & True Favorites* is a welcome addition to any home cook's kitchen!

Allrecipes Tried & True Cookies; Top 200 Recipes

Cookie lovers rejoice! Enjoy the world's best cookie recipes and invaluable baking tips and tricks that will turn anyone into an expert on preparing, decorating and sharing cookies. With over 230 cookie recipes, you'll find tried and true recipes for all your old favorites, and lots of new favorites you just haven't discovered yet!

Allrecipes Tried & True Quick & Easy; Top 200 Recipes

Great-tasting meals in minutes! This cookbook features delicious dishes that can be prepared in an hour or less, and are even organized by total cooking time for your convenience. Discover the joys of cooking without spending hours in the kitchen!

Allrecipes *Tried & True* cookbooks are available at select bookstores, by visiting our website at http://www.allrecipes.com, or by calling 206-292-3990 ext. #239. Watch for more *Tried & True* cookbooks to come!

For more information on Allrecipes and our *Tried & True* cookbooks, visit http://www.allrecipes.com today!

Allrecipes.com
524 Dexter Avenue North
Seattle, WA 98109 USA
Phone: (206) 292-3990, Ext. 239
Web: www.allrecipes.com

credits

the staff at allrecipes

Jennifer Anderson
Kala Anderson
Karen Anderson
Barbara Antonio
Emily Brune
Scotty Carreiro
Sydny Carter
Jill Charing
Jeffrey Cummings
Kirk Dickinson
Steven Hamilton
Blanca Hernandez
Tim Hunt
Richard Kozel

William Marken
Wendy McKay
Elana Miller
Carrie Mills
Bill Moore
Todd Moore
Yann Oehl
Matt Panken
Alicia Power
Ray Sotkiewicz
Judy St. John
Britt Swearingen
Esmee Williams
Krista Winjum

thanks

The staff would like to thank the following people whose comments and feedback have made this a better book: Brenda Hunt, David Quinn, and Hillary Quinn.